STOP

THE WAY TO BEGIN

MARIVIC QUIAZON

ISBN: 978-1-8381993-8-8

Stop... the way to begin.

When stopping is the only way to begin again, it's a radical step to take. Life can be overwhelming. Social media and the curse of the rat race take us to a place in life where we do not intend to be. We are weary and tired of the everyday routines that bring us nowhere. We go with the flow, and at the end of our years, looking back, we have no idea where the time went! If you want a new lease on life, it is necessary to stop. You can be at the crossroads of life, and you have paused your journey to consider which way you are going to take. Whatever choice you make will determine your life's destiny. What if you have already taken a course, a path which is taking you somewhere you never really wanted to go or become? Stop. It is a radical solution to begin again.

This book will both inspire and challenge you to look at your life and ask yourself, "Am I living my life with regrets or am I too busy to even notice?" Life is short and it is even shorter when we don't stop and take stock of what we are spending our years on. This book will convince you that if you do take the courage to stop, then you have just made the most important and wisest decision you can make with your life. Happy beginning!

Marivic Quiazon
Liverpool, England
www.mavicbooks.com

Dedication

This book is written for everyone who wants to learn the art of slowing down or how to stop in order to begin again.

To the exhausted and weary, and to those who have just had enough of the busyness of life, this book is for you.

Acknowledgment

I want to acknowledge Rowena Balmeo, my best friend and encourager, for arranging the layout of this book and creating all the illustrations and graphics that help to explain some of the thoughts laid out in each chapter. I also want to give credit to Microsoft stock photos for some of the pictures used throughout this book, including some of the online images used.

Table of Contents

Introduction

Have you ever felt like you have almost lived your entire life, yet still feel like you have not truly started to "live"?

If a new beginning is what your heart is looking for, then slowing down is not enough. You have to completely stop everything that's overwhelming you right now in order to begin again. It's never too late to start doing what your heart truly desires. There is only regret in the end if you fail to even try to start the journey meant for your life. How do you begin?

At the moment of writing this book, I have come to terms with what life is really all about. I have been an achiever all my life, blessed with talents that could take me anywhere I wanted in this life. I was first in my class from the very beginning of my elementary years. I was always the leader, top of the class, and won countless academic contests. I could go on and on about these achievements, but I feel that I would be wasting my time enumerating these meaningless endeavours. Meaningless compared to what truly is important in this life. This, I learned early in life. I was in high school, walking down the corridor on my way to my English class when it hit me so suddenly that I realized how nonsensical it all was. I wanted to take a different path. Looking at my direction, I knew then that I would be going in the path of a student who would hate to lose or miss the mark all the time. I remember getting one mistake in an exam and crying on my way home, while the rest of my classmates who got just a passing grade were on their way to cinemas or games or some kind of relaxation in the city, while I would be beating myself up for missing one question on the exam. I should get 100 percent all the time!

There, in that corridor, I told myself, I will not let myself go down that road and will try my best to not be swept away by the pressures of life. I was in my first year of high school! I went to teach children in squatter areas everywhere I could. I did tutorial classes and went to teach in Sunday school. I would be juggling between my studies and my service to God in the church. I was moving fast with everything I could do to make my life useful. This, I have done until I started entering what they call "the life of a career woman". I officially entered the "rat race" at twenty-one! I immediately forgot the pledge I made to myself that I will never let myself be swept away by the pressures of life. I found myself very busy with everything! It was so easy to fall into this "busyness" trap. But time flies so fast! Days and months could turn into years before you realize it's all gone! One day you will ask, "Where did all my years go?" You might be sitting at a doctor's office after a terrible diagnosis and ask yourself, "Whatever happened to my life?" Where did it bring me all these years? Is this it? Sometimes, it is at this point in our life that we begin to ponder about what we are doing with our life and where it is heading. When something untoward happens to us, we have to stop.

That's when you start to look back. When setbacks come, we take notice. When suddenly, we got sick or lost our job, we've got to pay attention. Stopping when getting overwhelmed will help you get your life back in balance. Rushing all the time will consume your years without even noticing it is slowly going. Days will turn into weeks and weeks into months and months into years. One day, when you look back, you won't even remember specific years in your life, years or months when you had amazing things to celebrate or family moments which you might have missed were all buried under the rubble of your life which was in a hurry all the time!

I wrote this book so that you don't end up with many regrets in life, especially if you are just starting out on your journey and building your dreams. It is chaotic out there if you don't watch out where you are heading. It is very easy to be swept away by the many offers which this life will try to lure you with. That is why I encourage you to learn to stop and think about your life. Where are you heading? Do you really want the direction you are going in this life? If when you wake up, you do not have the enthusiasm to begin your day, maybe it is time to evaluate your life. Maybe it is time for you to stop?

If when you wake up, you do not have the enthusiasm to begin your day, maybe it is time to evaluate your life. Maybe it is time for you to stop?

1.

Why stop

Our society is full of rushing and nonstop chatter. We are all having to endure an era of unprecedented information overload! We have become very impatient and no longer know how to wait. We run here and there like headless chickens, pretending we are busy all the time. It makes us feel good when we are busy, and our "to-do" list is full. Yet, you lay awake at night wondering if your life is really making any sense. Do we just exist, or is there more to life than just fulfilling the expectations society placed on us at each stage of our short life?

When everything going on in your life overwhelms you, it is time to stop. Some say we should slow down, but this can actually make matters worse. Slowing down is like testing the water to see if you can make it to the other side or not. Stopping is a radical way of forcing yourself to think about your next direction. It is like standing at a crossroad. It will be the time when you will make the most important choice of your life. That's why stopping is the way to begin.

We all need to stop! There is so much we can do when we only stop! We can only look back when we stop. We can only appreciate the moment when we stop. We can only introspect and find our whys when we stop. We can in fact truly live when we learn how to stop!

When was the last time you stopped what you were doing just so you can really feel the moment? When was the last time you stopped by the roadside and noticed a flower bloom for the first time? When was the last time you heard the ocean and really listened to its waves? When was it that you allowed yourself to be fascinated again? Can you remember when was the last time you felt like a child again, laughing freely, running barefoot on the sands and inspecting the beauty of each shell that you see? When was the last time you stopped everything, you were doing just because you wanted to think about your life and its direction? When was the last time you asked yourself whether there is a meaning to the life you have chosen to live?

Stopping will allow you to make an

inventory of your life's choices, where you landed in life, and to honestly investigate all that you have done and ask yourself: "Am I really happy with where I am? Am I just going with the flow of the society where I am? Do I really love doing what I am doing now? When you learn to stop, it is as if you are breaking into something extraordinary out of your ordinary existence. It will teach you to analyze your life and take stock of what you have, what is important in your life, and to check whether you have those around you. It will enable you to hit a "pause" button and say to yourself, "Hang on a second, should I continue where I am going, or should I reconsider my life's direction? Where am I going, and do I really want to go in this direction? Sometimes, in this life, it is easier to just go along with the flow of things. It is easy to get consumed with all the demands of life, even though some of these demands might not be necessary. We tend to procrastinate and just go on with the flow before realizing it is too late. Stopping will help us to confront these bad habits head-on and critically ask ourselves whether what we are doing is really making any sense. We only get one shot at life, and we do not have the luxury of unlimited time to keep making mistakes and playing with our lives. Knowing the direction we are taking and being sure about it is key to having a life that is going somewhere and not taking a chance with life. Our choices in life determine where we will find ourselves ten or twenty years from now. Life is too precious not to take seriously. Only one life and it will soon pass. Would you just watch it go by without a thought as to where it is taking you?

Stopping will help you pave the way towards the road you really want to take in life. It will help you to reflect on what makes you happy, the work that you really love to do, your passions, and your strengths. These should be the things that surround you each day and not the things which society forced you to take on. Society will have many impositions on us. It will try to dictate what we must be happy about or how we should live our lives, or what kind of house we should have or what kind of car we should drive. It will try to attract you into believing that what the trend is and what the majority of people are accepting and doing are also what you should do in your life. But these are unrealistic expectations being imposed upon us, not what our heart is truly beating for. We all have our own ideals in life, our own moments of joy and triumphs, and our own lonely days. We get upset about different things. We are individuals, and the path we want to take in life will be different from what others want to take. I believe that we should not be judged by the choices we made in life because no one knows us truly in this life except God. Other people are not in our shoes so we should not try to live up to their expectation. When we stop, we will be able to see through the filters of our lives, and we will be able to change course if necessary. What is stopping you from hitting your "pause" button?

"When was the last time you stopped what you were doing just so you can really feel the moment?"

2.

The rat race is killing us

Of course! It s manic Monday 😫
Get up!
Brush your teeth!
Take a shower!
Dress up!
Have breakfast or skip breakfast!
Drive, ride a bus, or take a train!
Work. Sit at your desk, whether it s the CEO's, manager's, or employee's desk, nursing station, or engineering depot!
Deliver by bike!
Drive, ride a bus, or take a train!
Go home!
Have dinner!
Watch TV!
Sleep!

Repeat!

They say that the most hated day of the week is Monday. It is the first day of the working week, and everyone will be rushing to go to work. The traffic will be horrendous, and horns will be sounding on every major road all around the world! It is Monday and the rat race begins. The rat race is a cliche. People use this to describe the daily scenario of every working-age person on the planet. You wake up to prepare to go to work, joining the morning rush hour. We then rejoin the same "rush hour" on our way home. We eat quickly and go to bed only to wake up again the next day doing the same thing we did on Monday over and over again. On and on, life goes on this way until retirement comes. This is the rat race. It seems like a dead-end existence for many of us. Most people wonder how they never noticed their years are all gone until they were sick in a doctor's clinic. With years of stress and work pressure etched all over their faces, each one looks away with an empty gaze. Distraction is the only hiding place for many. Entertainment numbs our pain and provides us with a momentary relief from our tiresome existence. We look outside and wish to escape the rat race we found ourselves in. But for most of us, it comes too late.

Why do we endure the rat race? For many people, it seems like the only way to exist. We each must pursue a certain dream. We started out with a noble intention. People naturally want to be happy and comfortable in life. Yet, in pursuit of happiness, we lost the very means towards this. We lost the meaning of life to some kind of system and expectation of the society we live in. We ended up living up to the expectation of others. It is as if our life is mapped out for us already at every stage. We must go to school, go to university and earn a degree, pursue a successful career, and before hitting 30, one must get married and have kids. Then the relentless pursuit of material things starts, when in comes the need for a mortgage and the furniture to put in it. Then the technology and stuff that makes life more convenient but at a price. We surrounded ourselves with so many things we don't really need but society and social media tell us we need them. The lifelong accumulation of possessions and "stuff" begins. This is the reason why we endure the rat race even though deep inside, we wanted to escape it.

Now, if we come to think of these things from a bigger perspective, we all, in this world, just live our lives on a tiny speck of dust suspended in the vast universe. We see this clearly illustrated to us through "the pale blue dot", a picture of the earth taken by Voyager on its way back to earth after years of taking photographs of our own solar system. There, in that picture, the earth looked just like a mote, a tiny speck of dust suspended in a sunbeam. What does that tell you and me? That at the end of the day, no matter how much wealth one amasses and how much power one has over the world or part of this tiny speck, we all live in a fragile world which could explode any time if one of the planets loses its own course or an asteroid decides to pass by the earth's orbit. Some people who are the "élites" of the world, we call them the "1" percent who owns 99 percent of the world's wealth, spend their lives plotting and conspiring to take a piece of that speck here and there which they will one day inevitably leave behind. Then in 30 to 50 years or three generations at the most, people will never remember they existed. The same is true with ordinary people like you and me. Time will surely come that our existence on earth is forever forgotten.

King Solomon wrote in his book called Ecclesiastes, that it's all vanity of all vanity. Everything is vanity and chasing after the wind. He was the wisest man who ever lived in his time. He was also very powerful and wealthy. Yet he said at the end of his life, that there is no meaning to all the achievements his life has accomplished. In the end he said that the conclusion of the whole matter is "Fear God and keep His commandments, for this is the whole duty of man."

I believe that people who hold on to possessions and try to accumulate for themselves, "stuff" in their names, are not truly free. Those "stuff" is their prison, and they live inside it. These people are very miserable inside. They know they are so consumed with themselves. This alone is a recipe for unhappiness. The opposite is true of giving away and helping other people. It is the recipe for true happiness because "real freedom" is when you can give it all away. If, when you look at all that you have accomplished and accumulated and can genuinely walk away from it all at a moment's notice, then, and only then, you are truly free and that none of those "stuff" possesses you.

If we look at our short life on earth as travelers, it will be easier not to hold on to things. We are literally transient visitors here. Time will come, the world will not even remember we passed by!

You are never freer than when you can give away things that you hold on to. The moment you can let go of what you hold, or that which takes hold of you, is the moment you have freed yourself.

So, freedom for most people is an illusion. I have only met very few people who are truly free in my lifetime. The look in these people's eyes, that's their distinguishing feature. It differentiates them from the rest. The way they talk speaks volumes about the freedom they have from the things they possess. It never possessed them.

How can we stay free? Look at this picture. The cave nebula, a diffuse nebula located in the constellation of Cepheus, is about 2,400 light years away, meaning, we are seeing it as if it was 381 BC! One light year is a staggering 6 trillion miles away. And this nebula is 2,400 light years away! How insignificant our time on Earth is compared to this reality!

Photo by Gareth Daggitt

Why am I telling you all this? Because this is what helps ground me. To know our place in the universe and how our life is just equivalent to a nanosecond existence in comparison to the immensity of space. This tiny earth is only like a mote of dust suspended in a sunbeam. Yet, God priced us with such significance that He sent His only Son, Jesus Christ, to come into our dimension so that we could understand His great love for each of us! What an awesome truth that the God who was from the beginning of time and who created all these came to become like one of us in order to save us from the mess we have created for ourselves.

That age-old sin which has separated us from God was dealt with through His death on the cross. The shedding of His blood has provided a way for all of us to escape the vanity of our existence. He came to set us free and give meaning to our lives. We only need to believe.

Are you getting tired of just existing and joining the everyday "rat race"? If you feel like you are getting fed up with your everyday routine, maybe stopping or pausing will help you to reset your life. It does not mean to leave your job straight away! It only means trying to find time in your schedule to reflect on where you are right now. It means to think deeply about where your life is taking you and if you are not where you wanted to be, maybe it is time to draw out a way of escape from the rat race you found yourself in. There are many ways to do this. The main thing is you have identified your need to stop. Then you can map out your way out. For some people, planning their way out could take a few years. Planning the details as to how you will begin once you decide to start   something to get out of your never-ending routines. In my case, I started with small steps. I was getting frustrated not being able to do more of the things I wanted in my life. I had to request extra annual leave just so I could stay longer in the mission field. I had to allocate and divide my time away for family, friends, and the work of the mission. Then, after returning from the trip, I had to re-enter the "rat race," doing the same thing again and again until the next planned trip. It was difficult and frustrating until I decided I could not live like this until retirement! I tried doing agency shifts for two years to see if this flexibility would help me do more of the things I love. Going on mission works in Asia, helping orphans and poor kids to have a better future and get them off the streets is where I want to spend most of my life, and it will not happen if I just go with the flow of how society wants everyone to live. After trying out doing agency shifts, I decided to completely stop being employed. I left my nursing job and started a nursing agency business with my best friend. Together, we entered this unknown world of business. We did not really know what we were doing, but we took the chance. It was a risk worth taking because it was a risk that would open possibilities for us to escape the rat race and be free to do what we love. It was not easy, it was very hard, and it was full of setbacks and failures. It was harder than being employed, but once we pressed through and fought our way out, we finally made it! It was something we will always be grateful for in this life!

Planning your way out will involve a lot of trial and error, but don't be discouraged by this. It will be so worth it if you can try to work your way out of the rat race. Start with simple steps like looking at your spending and seeing how you can make it better so you are saving more than you are spending. Look at investments and stock options. Read books and study other people who are successful and learn from their stories. Start developing habits that will help you become more organized and look at your daily routines to see if your daily habits are going to help you become the person you want to see in ten or twenty years. Work towards becoming that person. Habits make us become the person we want to be. It helps us develop our character and disposition in life. In business, one needs to be strong in character, and discipline is indispensable if you want to be successful.

If when you look at your life and you are happy where you are, then that is wonderful! The main thing is that you are happy and that you are doing exactly what you love to do in this life. Simplify your life, and you will be happier. Don't aspire to what other people are trying to achieve. Be who you are, live simply, and try not to make so many demands out of life if it is only to copy other people! Live your life as if it were your last day and try to make each day count. Remember, you don't really need all the things social media is flashing on your screen right now! If you think about it, we don't really need so many things to be happy in this life! You don't really need a bigger television or the latest car model this year or the upgrades which they will insist you need. Think before buying anything. Do what you love to do so it does not feel like you are "trapped" in a career which you are doing because you have to. Most of the time, people spend money on entertainment to distract themselves from the misery of having to do the job they don't love, so they momentarily forget about it. When you get up each morning, ask yourself whether you will be doing what you love. Be honest, and if the answer is yes, you are already on the right track, but if not, then maybe you need to stop and figure out how you can reset your life and start again doing what you love.

"If we look at our short life
on earth as travelers,
it will be easier not to hold on to
things. We are literally
transient visitors here. A time will
come when the world will not even
remember we passed by!"

3.

Hustle and bustle

The hustle and bustle of life overwhelms us. If we don't stop, we will be like running in a wheel, going with the flow of life's hustle and bustle. Years pass by quickly before anyone notices that they have all gone. We seem to be constantly in the "fast lane" of life. We rush all the time. Our "to do" list gets longer every day. Busyness becomes a comfort to many of us. People no longer have time to stop and notice what is going on around them. Going through the motions, we lose the ability to think deeply enough to analyse what is happening around us.

With all the entertainments and distractions of social media, we become apathetic and became more "inward" in our outlook. We lost our sense of community and sensitivity to the needs of others. Everyone becomes so absorbed in their own issues and problems that there is no more time for others. Because of this, people have become very lonely.

According to a 2021 study* conducted by a team of scientists in the UK, loneliness is a major public health concern which can raise a person's risk of death by 45%, more than air pollution, obesity, or alcohol abuse. The study was the first to assess how the environment can affect loneliness. It concluded that being with nature and connecting with other people on a more personal level significantly reduced feelings of loneliness.

If we are constantly busy, our body tries to deal with this by releasing a stress hormone called cortisol, which stays elevated when we do not stop working. This, in turn, will make us forgetful. It may cause brain fog or memory loss due to a constant increase in cortisol level which damages the brain cells in the hippocampus, the centre of brain memory.

Have you ever noticed how easily you forget things when you are too busy? Sometimes, the hustle and bustle of life can wreak havoc on our ability to concentrate. We lose the power to think critically, and we become almost like robots!

Busyness robs us of a much-needed time for rest and reflection. It also prevents us from spending quality time with our loved ones, who deserve our love and attention. Quality time spent with friends and family is the bedrock of a stable relationship. Rest is something we must do to give our weary bodies a much-needed break from the hustle and bustle of life. Without this, we are setting ourselves up for "burnout". When we reach this point, breakdown is inevitable. The ones close to us suffer the most when this happens.

How do we balance being busy and having time for what is important in life at the same time? I have written here three simple steps to help you start taking control over the hustle and bustle of life.

1. Learn to say NO! There is nothing wrong in recognizing that you cannot do it all! There is nothing to be guilty about declining a request if you really can't make it. There is nothing wrong about saying no to something you cannot possibly do for others. Remember this: No one can please everybody. Saying no frees you from the unnecessary burden of having to do tasks which you did not really want to do in the first place. Although it is hard to do when you start to let go of this bad habit of always saying "yes", you will in the end realize that saying no is one of the best things

you can do for yourself and others. Be honest with yourself and acknowledge your limitations. Others will appreciate this more than you think. Honesty is always the best policy.

2. First things FIRST! Ask yourself each day, what is important to you for that day? Learn the four quadrants of time management from the book "The Seven Habits of Highly Effective People" by Steven Covey. The first quadrant is what we do first; they are the urgent and important things. It could be a hospital visit to see your friend or someone you love. A phone call which cannot wait because it will affect your future

or a decision that must be made to know your next move. The second quadrant is what we make sure we put in our schedule and not set aside; they are not urgent, yet important. This can be taking your children out or watching their game. It can be time to spend with your mom or writing a thoughtful letter to your friend who is going through some difficulty. These appear less urgent, but they are important in our life. But because they are less urgent, we tend to set them aside and they become buried in the hustle and bustle of life. Before you know it, you are being robbed of this very important thing in your life. In fact, sometimes, we justify our busyness with "I'm doing this for them" mentality. But the sad thing is that we are losing "them" in the process. Before you know it, the very reason for your busy endeavours and pursuits, becomes the casualty of your "preoccupied" life. Always have time for the people that you love. They are the reason why you are working so hard. They need your time more than the "stuff" you try to shower them with. The third quadrant is what keeps most of us busy all the time! They are urgent but not important. Because they are always in your face, constantly calling for your attention, you end up being a slave to its bidding. The emails in your inbox call on you each day.

The shopping and washing greet your tired eyes every morning and demand your time to deal with them. They all appear urgent and must be done, yet they are not more important than your child waiting for you to spend time playing with them, or your friend waiting for your call. The last quadrant is what we sometimes spend so much time with each day without realizing it. Social media feeds distract us and catch our attention without knowing it. A friend sent a new post on Facebook, and you scroll down the photos and before you know it, you have spent the whole afternoon already browsing over the Facebook advertisements on your phone!

The messages and posts you feel you need to reply to are neither important nor urgent so they can wait. You can attend to them if you have extra time, but these should not take priority in your schedule. Learning to prioritize what you must do based on these four quadrants will help you find balance amid your busy schedule each day.

3. Take a BREAK! Do not feel guilty for not doing anything! The very essence of rest is not doing anything! Taking a break means taking a BREAK. Sometimes, I personally find it hard to rest and have a break too. To help me take a break, I make myself have a break. I must decide to shut

down. I must consciously make an effort to NOT DO ANYTHING! When we are constantly doing something, our brain does not know how to relax. It has been conditioned to be constantly thinking and working. But this is not good for our mental health. This is also not good for the people we love. The balance of life requires that we rest. God rested on the seventh day after He created everything. This should teach us something important. To balance life, there must be a rest from hard work. The beauty of taking a break comes from the renewal that we get from the rest we give our body and mind. Taking a break refreshes us and refocuses our attention. It helps us reflect on what we have been doing. It allows us to do our checks and balances. It reinvigorates our inner being and helps us to return to the joys of childhood. Allowing yourself to relax is the best thing you can do for yourself. Walk barefoot along the seashore, feel the softness of the sands, and breathe in the fresh ocean air. Nature has the power to heal our hurts and brokenness. Just by listening to the waves helps us to be at peace. It is a reassuring sound as if God is telling you, "Everything is going to be okay." Stroll down the forest, discover what's in the woods, gaze in wonder upon the stars above, wonder at the flowers as they bloom for the first time in the spring. Teach yourself to have a break from this artificial world and go back to nature. Take a break from it all. Have a lazy afternoon just reading your favourite book. Watch the sunset and spend time really listening to people you love. These things will give balance to your busy lifestyle, making sure you are not missing the ones that are truly important in life.

A friend of mine once wrote a poem after a road accident which shook her and woke her up from the fast-paced life she was living then. She has very kindly given her permission for me to include her poem in this book.

*The rushing, the stress, the
chaos of life in the fast lane,
that consumed you in the
fastest gear.*

*Days where you had no time
for the most precious people in
your life.*

*The time you let go in seeking
what you thought you must do
and sacrifice.*

*Sacrificed the calmness and
went into the storm, got
caught up in a whirlwind that
consumed you to the core.*

*When all you ever needed was
what you already had, you
sacrificed those precious
moments for something that
ultimately made you feel sad.*

*The moment it could have
ended, by someone doing that,*

speeding, rushing, a lapse of
concentration and gone just
like that.

Life has to be a journey, a
journey to be enjoyed, there is
no prize to the finish line,
except regret you didn't
appreciate things more.

Appreciate the moments,
appreciate the calm, appreciate
the kindness that touches from
afar.

Life in the fast lane is not the
place to be, I prefer to take my
time and appreciate things
with glee.

One day I won't be here to
appreciate it all, I need to step
back and enjoy the journey
more.

*The simple things in life far
outweigh the rest.*

*Enjoy the journey, not the
race, for today I have been
blessed.*

A Poem by Rachel Daggit

*"Always have time for the people that
you love. They are the reason why you
are working so hard. They need your
time more than the "stuff" you try to
shower them with."*

4.

The prison called 9-5

Are you a clock-watcher at work? Do you start counting the hours the minute you step into your office or cubicle? A 9-5 job has become our everyday prison. For most of us, we dread the start of a working week. We know we will be imprisoning ourselves in our 9-5 jobs and dreaming of our dream vacation to help us get through the day. A 9-5 job makes life very predictable. With this, we lose the excitement of everyday and settle for the tiresome repetitive jobs from 9 am till 5 pm. This makes us retreat into the "mundane". We lose our inspiration, and we no longer live with passion and purpose in life. We come to work and get by, surviving the day by watching the clock or daydreaming about our next break or time away from it all! This kind of life makes us feel frustrated and empty. We long for a more meaningful life. We look out of the window from where we work and wish we were doing something else. This is called the modern-day prison without bars. If you let your life continue this way, you will be surprised to realize that one day, you have used up all your years living inside this prison. It is never too late to start over again. Nothing in life is wasted if you keep trying until you find what you are looking for. How do you get out of this prison? The key is courage. Having the guts to try something new or start that one thing you have always wanted to do. It will not be easy, but it is better than living your life continuously pondering the "what ifs 'of your life. Don't be afraid! Go out there and throw yourself into that dream you have always imagined you would become one day. Try and keep trying. Never ever give up until you realize your dream. Don't settle for a mediocre existence. There is more to life beyond the 9-5!

How do you start? It is not going to be easy because by default, we all just want to stay where we are! We couldn't be bothered to get out of our comfort zone. We have all been programmed to live to work. In fact, if you think about it, each one of us was encouraged to go to school, earn a degree so we could work for some corporate businesses and on and on we live our lives as if on a treadmill until retirement. The conditioning is very strong so that the minute we try to test the waters and find that it is not how we imagined it, we retreat back to where we were and just dream again. But the problem with this is that we are not realizing that our years are going, and we are not getting any younger! If you keep delaying doing what you really love to do, the time will come that it might be too late for you, and you might lose your enthusiasm to try. You will end up retreating to the 9-5 life. You will look out from the same window where you work and dream and imagine the "what ifs" of your life yet again.

The first thing is to acknowledge that it is not going to be a smooth sailing ride. It will be harder in the beginning. Like everything in life, it is always the most difficult part to begin. Taking the first step is the key to starting out. Have a plan and think really hard about the kind of life you really want to have.

Plan how much you will need to start and save up as much as you can towards this. Diversify your money strategies, don't stick to just one way of savings or investing. When you are ready, just take the courage to go for it. If you don't try, you will never know if you can make it or not. I love a quote by a French explorer, Andre Gide who said; "Man cannot discover new oceans unless he has the courage to lose sight of the shore." This means that moving into the unknown requires us to take risks. It is not always guaranteed but the possibilities are endless, and you can only find out and see these possibilities if you try. So, I encourage you to take risks, to take your chance into the unknown world beyond the 9-5 and prepare yourself to be surprised with what is out there! Who knows what is waiting for you and your family if you give it a try?

To me, the most exciting life is a life that is not afraid to take risks. Life is all about taking risks. When we go to work and drive our car, we take the risk of driving on the road without the guarantee of reaching our destination with 100 percent safety. We all know this, but we still take the risk. When we ride in an airplane, we take the risk of being vulnerable up there at 42,000 feet! You took the risk when you decided to accept the job you have right now. Nobody knows what it's like before they embark on their journey. Life is like this. It is a long journey with lots of unknown destinations and unknown people along the way. Yet, we are all on this journey, taking our chances, discovering new things, meeting new people, learning lessons after every mistake and so life, this journey goes on and on until it's our time to stop. I don't think life has a destination because some travelers could stop the journey suddenly. Some can go so far, some don't. Some have only managed to travel a short distance and had to stop. Some go on and get very far, some go halfway in the journey and then finish. Life is a journey to be enjoyed and cherished. Each of us will have a different story to tell on this journey. Don't let society dictate your own story. Don't let them set for you how you will travel in this life. Society has certain norms and expectations that it asks from every person who lives in this world. Don't fall into this trap. Be brave to go the other way. Go and try another way because there is always another way to live your life. It does not have to be this way for everybody. You don't live to go to work. You don't live your life to buy those things social media is telling you to buy. You don't live your life to do exactly the way they map it out for you. Live freely and know your purpose. It is a beautiful journey. Each of us has a path we will choose to walk on. Don't let anyone tell you it is the wrong path you are taking. Be at peace with your Maker. Be sure of your life's purpose. Go out there and live your life differently from the rest of them! No one has the right to tell you are doing it wrong. Live your life! Do what you love and enjoy every moment. Because you will only live once, and your life is only short. Do you want to spend all your years watching from the window at your workplace and dreaming about your next holiday, watching the clock and wishing it would go quickly because you want the day to end and want to get out?

If this is you, it might be that you need to stop. You might need a "pause" to your daily routines. Find time to sit down and check on what you really want to do. Do you want to continue the daily grind and live like the majority of the people who lived on this planet? Or do you want to take your chance outside of this 9-5 prison and discover the freedom and the excitement of living the life you truly wanted to live?

"It is never too late to start over again.
Nothing in life is wasted if you keep trying until you find what you are looking for."

5.

I don't have a life!

Have you ever heard this phrase from an exhausted friend? "I don't have a life!" We hear this when our colleagues sometimes exclaim that all they do is work, work, work! Then, we will hear comments like, "Go out there and have a life! Go out on vacation, go and have fun!" These are the common cries of many who are bored with their jobs and are desperate for something new to do!

How do you define "life"? Something with life in it will be bursting with purpose. It is going to be full of goodness to benefit another life. A plant or a tree with life will be full of vitality and freshness. Life is vigorous and blooming. It has joy and purpose. There is meaning to its existence. When one is alive, there is satisfaction and happiness.

In contrast, if one says he or she does not have a life, this can mean this person is finding life boring and repetitive. The daily routines become a drag, and the person wishes to do something else. Life has lost its vitality and purpose and is no longer driving the daily toil. This has removed meaning from daily existence and has become a "must do" in order to survive. When life becomes like this, one loses inspiration, and the joy of living is gone. When one comes to this point, it is a desperate cry for a new start. One must stop. Stop the routine. Stop the flow of the ordinary and let something extraordinary comes out of it. It becomes necessary to pause. To think and reflect on life and where it is taking you. It is time to ask the hard question. Do I love what I am doing? Am I excited about life and where it is taking me? This is the best time to STOP. When every day starts to overwhelm you and you no longer see the reason why you are alive, it is time to stop and begin again.

Your life must count for something. One life is all we have. What we do with this life is our choice. There will be many appealing choices, many offers of wealth, success, fame, all kinds of pleasures. There will also be options to live it differently. To make your life count, to live your life making a difference in the life of another. If one chooses to go for the offer of wealth and success, fame or pleasure, there can be momentary satisfaction and "fun" from all that it has to offer. This can be exciting at first, you might get intoxicated with all the highs it gives you. But when all the smoke is gone from this "high" life, what is left will define reality for you, your "real life". When all the fun goes away, looking at your life, what can you say it did? Having a "life" is not being successful in this life or amassing all the wealth you can have. Having a "life" means having a purpose which makes you wake up each morning excited to live another day because you know your life is making a difference to another human being. Having a life means you are living the life designed for you, the life you are meant to live. Your life's purpose, your life's mission is why you were born. This kind of "life" is different than all the other lives we see around us. This life is a satisfying life. This life is full of zest and vitality because it is oozing joy and happiness and purpose. This life knows it matters to a child or a parent or a friend. This life knows it makes the world a better place. Having a life means living your life for something every day. It is waking up for a cause bigger than your own life. It is a life which does not live for itself alone but for others, making other people's lives better and leaving a footprint of joy and contentment everywhere it goes.

If you feel like you are in prison with

your job and not free to live the life you wanted, why are you staying? What is keeping you from trying to live your life differently and making your life count? Have a long look at your routines. Check how you feel about your everyday. Is your daily routine making you want to stop and do something different? Are you itching to go on holiday again the moment you return to work? Do you often daydream about doing something else while at work? If your answer is yes, then you need to stop and begin your life again. You need a reset!

A reset button is a life-saving feature of every machine or computer. When we get stuck and have made so many mistakes and the computer keeps on playing up, we appreciate the reset button! Hitting it makes us very happy because we can start again as if nothing happened. We can correct our mistakes and begin better. We all need a reset button in this life. There are mistakes to learn from and regrets to redeem. Sometimes life can be so chaotic and messy, we want to stop and start anew. We want a reset. Imagine if we could just press this reset button every time we want to start over again! Well, I know maybe you are thinking it is not that easy in real life, but the truth is you can always choose to stop and reset your life. You can always start again! What you need is the courage to begin again.

How do you begin? It could be your long-held dream buried under the rubble of past mistakes. It could be a simple step to reconcile with a loved one, or someone you have hurt or who has hurt you in the past. It could be a mountain of "to do" lists or your life's "bucket list" that you keep on putting aside. It could be picking up a long-lost dream and reviving it. Whatever it is, you can find the courage to begin again if you learn to stop. Once you stop, you can figure out your life's direction, you can start to reflect on whether you are really doing what you love and whether you are really at a place in life where you want to be. Only then you can take the first step towards your new direction and begin again.

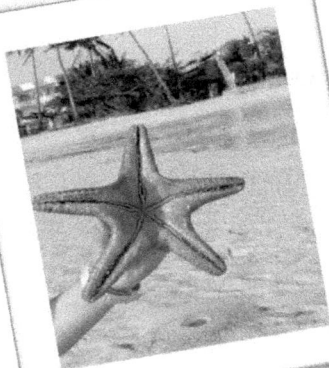

"Stop the routines. Stop the flow of the ordinary and let something extraordinary comes out of it."

6.

Learning to reflect

Learning to reflect is an art. As with everything in life, the art of reflecting on your life and the paths you have taken can be learned.

Why learn to reflect? Reflecting on your life's choices helps you to consider your journey and enables you to make the necessary adjustments if needed. Reflecting also helps you to apply the lessons learned from mistakes you have made in the past. It helps you to refocus your life. Reflecting on the steps you are taking can have a very positive impact on your whole journey in life. It will reassure you if you're on the right track and will help you to go back and retrace your steps if you need to correct or make up for something which you have ignored or lost along the way. For example, if at some point in your life, you have become so busy and preoccupied, making you spend less and less time with the people who truly matter to you, upon reflecting over your life, you can do some checks and balances. You can return and try to redeem those times when you hardly spent time with your family. You can try to recover lost moments by trying to make up for those lost opportunities. Reflection will help you to begin again if necessary. There are many times in our lives when we neglect what is important because of the pressing "urgent" matters competing for our attention. During highly stressful times in our lives, it is easier to slide into just ignoring the important things in life like our relationship with family and friends, spending time with your spouse or your children, visiting your parents, and spending quality time with a friend who is sick. When we are busy, it is very difficult to set aside time to reflect on what is happening or what you are doing with your life. We must, therefore, try to deliberately set aside a time for us to reflect on the events of our lives and the direction it is taking.

How do you teach yourself to reflect? I always choose a tranquil and quiet place to reflect. A peaceful walk along the seaside can do wonders to naturally get you in a "reflection" mode! The sound of the ocean has the power to calm your mind and soothe your weary soul. When you listen to the waves, the sound of water, and the feel of the ocean breeze upon your face will automatically teach you to reflect on your existence. A beautiful and secluded garden can also be a great place to teach yourself to reflect. Listen to the birds sing or allow yourself to appreciate the flowers as they start to bloom. The scents of the various flowers in the garden and the colors of the leaves will help you to reflect on your life. It will help you to listen and be silent. When you stop thinking, you will learn to listen to your inner voice. Taking time to be quiet is crucial to reflection. Only when we are quiet can we truly listen to our conscience. Only when we are silent can we truly hear our own thoughts and listen to the voice inside our soul. Silence is key to reflection. Reflection is like looking back at yourself in the mirror. When you look in the mirror, it reflects "you" back. You see yourself and notice if something is not quite right with the way you look. It shows you if you have some dirt on your face or if your makeup is not the best and this helps you to make adjustments. This is the same as reflecting on your life's journey. Somehow, learning to reflect is learning to stop and look at yourself. This is what we do every day when we look in the mirror. We check on how we look and adjust our look accordingly until we are happy. Reflection does the same thing. We make adjustments if after reflecting on what we are doing, we realize we need to make some adjustments. We learn to affirm our joys and get reassurance if we know we are on the right path in life. Our heart tells us because deep inside, we know if we are truly happy in the life we have chosen to live. We also find comfort and assurance when we know that we are doing the right thing. The opposite is true if we are not at peace with what is happening in our lives. When we reflect, we feel a kind of "chaos" inside our heart and mind. There is no peace. There is restlessness. We can then allow ourselves to retrace our steps, to look back and make the necessary changes or adjustments to take us back on the right path. Learn to listen to the whispers of your heart. It might not agree with what you think is practical at the moment, but your inner voice can only rest in peace when it knows you are doing the right thing, and you are at the right place at the right time.

Learn to reflect. Have a notebook of your thoughts and reflections. Write a poem or write whatever worries you have and allow yourself to reflect on those. Tear down the pages once you have finished writing and reflecting back on all your worries. They are not meant to stay inside your thoughts. The main thing is you look back at them and this is what teaches you what to do next. Trust your inner voice. Listen in silence as you try to dig deeper into your soul. Listen to what it wants and do not ignore what it tells you to do.

"A peaceful walk along the seaside can work wonders to naturally put you in a reflective mode! The sound of the ocean has the power to calm your mind and soothe your weary soul."

7.

How to think deeply in a superficial world

━━━━━━━━━━━━

How do we learn to think deeply when everyone around us is content with the superficial? We all suffer from information overload, and the constant barrage of social media feeds and adverts on our phone's conditions our brains to "look" only, but not to "think" about what we see. Because of how fast all this information comes to us, we lose the ability to think. Scrolling over the pictures and videos on our phone screens trains our minds to be impatient and become less responsive. We become shallow. We rarely stop and critically analyze the information presented to us because new ones come on the screen in less than a minute after we read one piece of information. The brain has no time to think about what we saw.

This kind of mental conditioning is very subtle; we hardly know it is happening. The reels and shorts we are being trained to watch on YouTube, Instagram, and TikTok are slowly making our brain want to watch only low-content feeds. This, in turn, makes us very impatient because our brain becomes so used to scanning through short feeds of information which keep on changing every few seconds. The result: everyone is becoming very impatient. Everyone becomes passive consumers. We passively consume all the information being fed to us day in and day out without thinking about it. The whole of society is being trained to think superficially. This is a very sad reality.

Thinking deeply is very important for our health and mental well-being. It is in learning to think critically that we keep our mind healthy and active. We don't just look as if in a daze over the information we are seeing or hearing. We stop to analyze it and weigh it in order to form our own judgment about what we see. This helps us to form our own opinion about issues and problems outside our own world. We will not be susceptible to outside influence or suggestion so easily if we learn to be critical deep thinkers. If you think about it, the majority of what we are watching online is meant for us to just "watch" without thinking. I hardly see any program which encourages a healthy debate about the many controversial issues our society is facing nowadays. Most of the time, "expert" opinion will be presented to us, and we are expected to just accept it as the conclusion. Hardly do we see any debate about issues that matter to our lives. If we do not do our own research about a certain subject or news, we are bound to believe whatever information is being introduced to us without analyzing it.

How do we learn this skill again? It can be a challenge as we live in this internet age. We need to be proactive and to consciously decide to relearn the skill again.

Pause and Think

To learn to think deeply, we must learn to pause and think. Pausing forces, you to consider and evaluate what you are hearing or seeing. It teaches you to think about something. When scrolling over the ads and information over our phones, the tendency is to keep scrolling for the next one. This is causing our brains to be conditioned, and eventually, we become like robots. People every day stare at their phones and scroll down unconsciously because it almost becomes an addiction to feel our phones in our hands and scroll down on the apps aimlessly. What we are being trained in doing this is superficiality. We take things at face value and so we become superficial thinkers, going with the flow and not caring whether the information is real. If we take everything at face value, we will never learn their authenticity. We then lose interest in researching the information. We no longer test anything. We unconsciously believe whatever is on the news without thinking whether this is true information. Most people lose the ability to form their own opinion and just parrot the opinion of whatever the news or media outlets try to put out there for mass consumption. Listen to what you are saying when in conversation with your friends and family. Analyze your own opinion and ask yourself, "Is it really my own opinion or thoughts, or is it what I have been hearing or being told in the news or what I have been reading on Twitter or Instagram? Without critical thinking, our society will end up being manipulated unconsciously. This will include you! Forming the habit of thinking deeply is key to protecting your own freedom to think for yourself. To analyze and judge information and then draw out your own thoughts about an issue. This will also keep your mind active. To research and test all information, one must take time to pause and think. Reading is the critical mind's best friend. Try to be a good reader. Make it a habit to read books. Reading can help widen your perspective and you will learn to think critically. When you read, you are learning how others think and how others view life. Reading also gives you time to learn to pause and think about what you read, compare it with your own thoughts and make your own decision about the subject.

Be a deep thinker. So much in this present world is superficial. We need to regain this ability which distinguishes us from animals. Our ability to think critically and analyze what we hear and see will enable us to think deeply in this superficial world. Engage in deep conversations with your friends and people older than you are. The older generation has so much to teach us. They have been on the road before. They have wisdom in life which we can apply to our own struggles and troubles. Practice talking to strangers. Start a conversation with someone at the bus stop while you wait for your bus or train. Be aware of your surroundings and learn to watch people. I love people watching because it helps me to understand individuals and learn from their body language and expressions. When I watch people as they pass by, I am learning to appreciate variety and differences in what I am seeing. Each person is different, and I learn to respect each individual as a person with their own values and preferences. This helps me think more deeply about people and society as a whole.

Regaining the ability to think deeply takes time and practice. If you set out to do this, you will develop mental capacity which can set you up to succeed and be ahead of your peers. When everyone around you is just scrolling down on their phones and getting entertained, you will be solving real problems and discovering new ways of dealing with people's difficulties in life and being paid for it! You will not be someone who just believes what is out there, but you will be someone who analyses and critically checks the information before taking it in. Think deeply and you will not live in a superficial world.

> *"People stare at their phones and unconsciously scroll down every day because it has almost become an addiction to have our phones in our hands and aimlessly scroll down on the apps."*

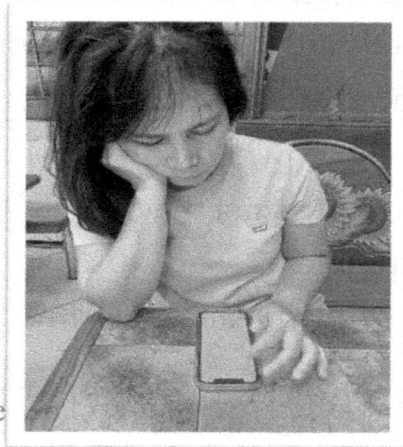

8.

Finding your way back

Looking at where our society is right now, it feels like we have gone so far from the calm and peaceful existence our grandparents used to enjoy. If you ask those who have lived before the internet era, they will tell you how different it was back then. How time felt slower and how they seemed to have time for everything. They will describe to you the joy of their childhood running barefoot in their backyard, climbing trees and enjoying games with other kids on the block. They will tell you the time when they could inspect every insect crawling in their gardens. They have memories of their mom and dad reading them bedtime stories and they can still remember the smell of their grandma's cookies! How different our existence is nowadays! We seemed to have forgotten how to slow down and stop to smell the roses. Most of us are living in the fast lane of life. Everyone's byword is "I just don't have the time!"

How can we find our way back? How do you return to the joy of living rather than living just to survive? How do you find your way back to return to what it used to be? Perhaps we won't be able to return completely but we can still recapture the moments and try to find some resemblance of a peaceful and contented existence, the way life should always be.

Let us start by re-tracing our steps. When I was a little girl, this was the trick I have remembered well when I was competing to win our famous **"Hampas Palayok."** This game takes the contestant blindfolded towards the hanging pot filled with goodies and the aim is to be able to return to it and hit the pot open, releasing all the goodies. The problem is, you will be blindfolded so you won't remember the exact location nor the distance of the pot once you are taken back to the starting line. The organizer will, however, take you from the starting point to where the pot is and let you feel the hanging pot with your stick. My trick was to count my steps back and carefully re-trace my steps so that I know how many steps will be needed to get to exactly where the hanging pot was! I always win the game!

How do we begin to re-trace our steps to find our way back? First is to revisit our childhood memories and remember how easy it was for us to laugh! This will sound silly but the first step to finding your way back is to learn to be a child again! We can learn so much from a child. Watch the way a child looks at everything for the first time. Learn from their curiosity and how easy it was for them to be happy. Children are the most authentic people on earth! They always tell you the truth! They don't know how to pretend so everything about them is real. Children do not worry about anything, and this is something we must relearn. To be carefree and relaxed. Worrying ages us and makes us sicker. Yet our problems are not solved by worrying. Going over problematic issues again and again and thinking about it and rehearsing about what we should have done will not change our situation. Jesus said, "Which of you by worrying can add a single day to his life's span?" This is so true, isn't it? If we learn to live only one day at a time, we will save ourselves a lot of trouble!

The art of relaxing is important. When we relax, we set aside our chores and "to do" list and consciously make an effort to relax and feel good about the moment. We take it easy and try to forget our worries. Relaxing is an art. We need to learn to develop this especially if we are, by nature, "doers". I used to find it hard to relax because I am naturally active and constantly want to be on the go and doing something all the time. But I realized that whether I keep on doing it and whether I stop and relax for a time, the things I need to do will always be there. There will always be something to do! I don't think there will ever be a day when we will have nothing to do! We must learn the ability to relax!

Another important thing we need to learn is the ability to let go. This is indispensable to living freely and happily. Children can forgive very quickly, and they never hold grudges. They forget ill feelings easily and this is what keeps them free. Let us learn from the children. Discover the inner child within you and learn to laugh again! Be a child from time to time. Loosen up! The world will still be here even if you pause for a moment and take a break. It is not all up to you. I have learned this from my mentor when I was just starting out as a missionary. I was very passionate and aggressive at the time, still young and full of dreams! One day, in one of our mentoring sessions, I kept going on and on about how the burden was too heavy for me and how the task is so big and there were so many things I needed to start and do in the mission field! He listened very patiently to me and just smiled after I said everything I wanted to say. Through my tears, he told me in a very thoughtful way, "It is not all up to you." That was the most important advice I received then. I needed to hear that. When I thought the whole world was on my shoulder, I had to realize that it is not all up to me! Let go of the burdens that are not meant for you to carry. Learn to take things one at a time. Let go of the things you cannot control and live freely like a child. Each day, count your blessings and think of one reason to smile. Laugh at silly things and give time for yourself to listen to others. Play with your kids. Go out in nature and walk barefoot on the grass or sands at the sea. Live your life with gratitude each day, being thankful that you are still alive and free. No one knows about tomorrow so take time to live just for today. Appreciate the moment. Learn to listen. Learn to wait.

The next step is to revisit your friends and return to the people you love. By this I mean to genuinely give them importance again. I know that you are with them every day. Perhaps you talk to them and deal with them on a regular basis. But, has your busy lifestyle and the pressures of work and life forced you to set them aside or to put them as your last priority because you have to deal with more "urgent" matters each day? When was the last time you were really present in the conversation with your wife or husband or a friend? Do you also play with your phone while eating out on a date with your loved ones? When playing with the kids, are you really present and enjoying the moment or are "more" important things at work occupying your mind? Sometimes it can look like we have it all together. Our life can "appear" perfectly on the outside but "crumbling" on the inside. Have we left the people in our lives who are truly important, in pursuit of a successful career? Are you truly happy with your life? Are there things left unsaid? Are you harboring future regrets in your life? Return to your loved ones while you still can and embrace them back in your life. Revisit your friends again and listen to them this time. Really listen to how they are doing. Hear what they are saying. Be present.

The third step is to have a break from technology. This will be a radical step to take because we are surrounded with technology wherever we go. We have them all around us at home, at work, at school, at shopping malls and even at parks and recreation centers! It almost feels like it's impossible to get away from it! But it is not. It is not impossible to get away from it all. You will need willpower to do this. But you can!

Set a day each week where you will shut down all technology around you. Perhaps it will be easier for you to go out in nature and deliberately not take the phone with you or turn it off for the duration of your time away. You can also try to leave your phone outside your room at night. You have to re-train your mind and your hands not to hold and look at your phone. You will notice how much of an addiction this technology has become. It is surprising how much hold our phones have on us.

Have you ever noticed yourself panicking when you forgot to bring your phone or accidentally left it somewhere? Losing our phones has become our worst nightmare! The fear and the panic in people's faces when they lose their phones speak for themselves! To find your way back, you will need to deliberately leave technology behind from time to time. You will not be able to find balance in this life if you are a slave to technology. We ought to control it rather than let it control us. Now, re-learn to watch time pass by. Sit on a bench in the park and watch people. Do something without rushing. Take your time to eat, enjoying each bite. Listen to your favorite music. Walk barefoot on the grass and feel the ground beneath you. This is called grounding, and it has been scientifically proven to help you relax and improve your sleep. Go on! Ditch your shoes and go back to the beauty of a simple existence. Feel the earth beneath your feet and connect with the natural world as you embrace the freedom of going barefoot. Whether walking along a sandy beach, strolling through dew-kissed grass, or simply padding around your own home, the sensation of barefoot movement can be grounding and invigorating. With each step, you can experience a heightened awareness of your surroundings and a sense of liberation from the confines of footwear. Embracing the simplicity and sensory experience of being barefoot allows you to truly connect with the present moment, setting aside the constraints of modern life and indulging in the simple pleasure of feeling the earth beneath you.

Once you have done these three simple steps, everything will fall into place again. You will trade the chaos of your life for a peaceful and quiet retreat. Your hectic life will find its balance, and you will know that you have found your way back when you are laughing again, and your smile has returned.

"Live your life with gratitude each day, being thankful that you are still alive and free. No one knows about tomorrow so take time to live just for today. Appreciate the moment. Learn to listen. Learn to wait."

9.

The art of slowing down

Slow down. Just before we completely stop, we slow down. This will be the first step to learning how to stop. If you slow down but do not plan to stop at some point, life will again be moving towards the mundane, though in a slower phase. But we will talk about learning the art of slowing down as preparation for stopping completely so you can begin again. Slowing down is an art. It is something we learn to do. It is also a choice that we make each day. If we are driving fast and we see a hazard on the road, our right foot automatically hits the brake pedal to slow down the car. Life can be the same. We have an innate tendency to want to slow down when feeling overwhelmed. Maybe because within us is a built-in protective mechanism to prevent us from reaching a breaking point. Learning the art of slowing down is easy. You only need to begin.

Each day, schedule a pause in your routines. Use this time to reflect on your day and to be thankful. Have a notebook to write down your thoughts. Choose a quiet spot in your workplace to do this. Have a quiet room in the house for reflection. If you can, go for a walk during your break time and if near the sea, walk by the seaside and let your mind wander freely. Doing this will help you to build up a habit to deliberately slow down your life's pace.

When your mind is worrying and thoughts are rushing inside you, learn the power of deep breathing. Take a deep breath and let your worries go as you breathe out. Deep breathing relaxes your muscles and indirectly relaxes your mind and emotions. Do this regularly until it becomes a part of your daily routine.

Learn to take things slowly. Eat slowly. How many times have you been rushing to eat? Savor the flavors of your food and enjoy the fellowship you are having with your loved ones while eating. Learn to listen more and talk slowly. Try to talk less but take time to observe and feel. Feel each moment.

Don't let it just pass by. There is power in listening to each moment, cherishing it and celebrating its joys. These are God's gifts to us. We have these moments every day. You only need to take time to notice them. If you are always in a hurry, you will not notice these moments. It will just pass you by.

Build a habit of meditation. Meditate on the goodness of God in your life. He always sees you through in every situation. Remember His faithfulness to you. Each morning, take time to pray and thank God for everything. Thank Him for the joys in your life and His blessings. Be grateful for your freedom and comfort because many others in the world do not have these same luxuries. I consider these two things' luxuries because in other parts of the world, people are still fighting for their freedom, and many are poor and do not even have the simple comforts of life. So be thankful for everything. When I am in the mission field, I am always reminded of how many blessings we take for granted in the west. Living among the tribal people made me reflect on these many blessings. The simple comfort of a nice bed or a clean toilet is something to be thankful for. The freedom we sometimes ignore is something so precious to those who are born without this. In North Korea, people do not even have the internet! They are not allowed to know what is really going on outside of their own country. They don't have the freedom to speak about what they think or how they feel. They don't have freedom to choose or decide about their lives.

Everything is decided by the state. How they work, dress, eat and even think is dictated to them. They can only dream of what we have. So, learn to be grateful for your blessings in life.

Retire from the chaos of your life. Tune out the sounds from the world outside and go to your secret place to retire from the world each day. It can be a bench in your back garden or a favorite corner in your house. It could be the seaside. Bring yourself to your favorite place and relax and unwind after a hectic day. This is your happy place. This is where you allow yourself to be free from the day's troubles and only happy thoughts are allowed.

Slowing down is about appreciating the moment and times when we are forced to stop the routines of life… how times like this help us reflect on life and consider our journeys. When we are so occupied with the demands of life, we do not have the chance to think deeply about life and give time to what is important. So, if suddenly you found yourself without work or you need to stop, appreciate this break and thank God for this brief time of rest which you won't otherwise have if work is always there.

Slowing down can do wonders for your weary soul. It automatically relaxes you. It helps put things in a more balanced perspective. It can be learned, and you can one day form the habit of slowing down. Once you have taken the simple steps to slow down, you will then master the art. It will give you much pleasure to see your life slowing down. Look back with joy at the journey you have traveled so far. Life is not a race. It is a beautiful journey to enjoy. It is a journey with lots of different stops. You must learn to stop when life asks you to. Tarry a little because life can show you amazing lessons at every stop. The journey should be celebrated and savored. You can only do it by learning the art of slowing down. Slow down when your body is telling you to slow down. Slow down when inside you, you are crying out for a break. Slow down when everything around you wants you to speed up. SLOW DOWN.

"We have an innate tendency to want to slow down when feeling overwhelmed. Maybe because within us is a built-in protective mechanism to prevent us from reaching a breaking point."

10.

The perils of convenience

Convenience can sometimes be our downfall. We have been conditioned to embrace societal change in the name of convenience. Advancements in technology have been sold to us because of the promise of convenience. We used to have televisions without remote controls. When the remote control was invented, couples ended up fighting for control. Before this, the wife happily changed the channel manually for the husband and the husband happily changed the channel for the wife. When the remote control arrived, things changed dramatically! Before, families happily watched television together; now, each room has its own television screen, and even the kitchen has a television! Families seldom talk to each other because each one would rather scroll down on their phones than talk to each other during mealtimes. Then came Alexa and Siri, and now most of us could not live without them! We used to dial up for the internet; now, if we wait for a few seconds for Wi-Fi connections, we are already getting restless! With the offer of more and more convenience, we have become slaves to technology. This, in turn, teaches us to be impatient. It disconnects us from people around us, and we no longer know how to wait and think. We ask Google for anything under the sun instead of trying to remember or think to find the answer. It is indeed convenient to ask Google because the answer comes in seconds, but the danger of this is that we are being conditioned to no longer think about anything! This can slowly remove our ability to think critically and to analyze any information we receive. All these are happening because we love the convenience which technology brings to us. Yet, we do not realize the perils this seemingly innocent convenience is bringing to our lives. Before we know it, we have already become accustomed to being convenient, and it is harder and harder to give it up.

Convenience can make us less and less able to take on hard challenges in life. It makes us complacent. It makes us an easy target for manipulation and suggestion. When we are convenient, it is easier for us to just go along with the flow of things. We find it hard to give it up because we have gotten used to the comfort it gives us. Even when this means losing something as precious as privacy, we have come to a point of being willing to even give it up for the sake of convenience. We did not mind if we are being spied upon or monitored by all the cameras everywhere, as long as we are convenient. Convenience somehow makes life more bearable, and henceforth we do not feel the need to pause or stop and consider. We do not reflect and think about life and its direction. But when suddenly our convenience is interrupted, we take notice and begin to think. We very rarely stop and think about life when it's all going well. But when something happens and setbacks come in, we are forced to stop and evaluate our life's priorities and its direction. This is sometimes necessary to allow us to review our mistakes and to reflect on what we are doing. The trials of life help us to be vigilant and enable us to rethink our life's values, giving us time to do an inventory of all the choices we made. It teaches us not to be complacent.

When life is convenient, we should not be so at ease that we forget to reflect and consider our ways. Living life without purpose can be frustrating and gives one a feeling of emptiness. Though convenient, life is empty, and joy is absent from the heart.

"We very rarely stop
and think about life when it's all going well.
But when something
happens and setbacks come in, we are forced
to stop and evaluate our life's priorities
and its direction."

11.

The power of being authentic

Authenticity is so rare, we had to look closely to find it. Being authentic is an attractive trait. When one pretends, people tend to shy away from them. We are drawn towards people who are real and genuine. Deep inside all of us is a repulsion to all things fake and unreal.

Real beauty comes from being authentic. Our eyes search for it and rest in its beauty. This is the reason why we love staring at the ocean or gazing over the majestic mountains. Our mind knows they are real. It is beautiful to behold because there is no pretension in nature. It is all natural. Authenticity lives in variety. No copycats are considered beautiful because somehow, we know they are not genuine.

It can be very tiring to try to be like someone else. Social media puts pressure on us to be like the celebrities or influencers they showcase on their platforms. But this can be exhausting and following these "idols" can eventually make you lose your own identity. This is tragic and sad. To find peace and rest from all this, you must accept yourself and look at life from a healthier and realistic perspective.

There's beauty in variety, and the reason why you are beautiful is that you are different. There is no one else like you in this world, and when you copy someone else, you are losing that beauty. What social media does and TikTok influencers do is try to persuade you to follow them and be like them. If you fall for this, you will lose the uniqueness of being you. Real beauty is being authentic. Being real and true to yourself. When you are different, that's when you are beautiful.

Curating your life to present only the "good" part on social media platforms is pretension. This can be very tiring to maintain. This also gives out the wrong message to others and impacts people negatively. Those who are otherwise happy and content with their lives suddenly "feel" bad about their life after seeing glamorous posts of one's travels and "seemingly" high life existence. On the other hand, the one curating all these posts knows deep inside, it is all for a show. One goes to places to take photos for posting on social media and misses the joy of travels and experiences. This can one day take its toll on the person. Becoming real and aiming to be true to yourself is liberating. It can help you to find true freedom and joy in life. The power of being authentic also radiates from the relationship we form with others. Our relationships will be stable and will be based on a genuine foundation. There are no secrets to hide. There is no need to pretend, and therefore one is free and happy to be who they are with each other. This authenticity is powerful.

Being real is being who you are. Staying

true to yourself and not trying to be someone else. The power of authenticity lies in the fact that one is dealing with something genuine. This in itself is very restful because the need to hide anything is eliminated from the equation. When one tries to pretend or hide something, there is always the tendency to try to maintain the false impression given initially, and this can be very exhausting. To live life in pretension is like living in prison. You are not free to be who you are, and you have to pretend to be accepted. Many times, this is where we get it wrong. People prefer to have someone who is authentic and real. It is tiresome to pretend to be someone other than who you really are. Let go of this tendency to hide your true self and just be yourself. Embrace your uniqueness and be at peace with your own identity. Learn to rest in this reality.

In nature, we see how beauty is found in its authenticity. Nature is always true and genuine. You don't see anything unreal among the trees or flowers, though they look so proud and confident in their beauty. Animals are always true to themselves and act as they are. Everything in nature lives up to its potential because they all follow their own design. Sometimes, in our attempt to be like someone else, we are losing our own identity, our own "design" or purpose in life, and so we don't fulfill our life's destiny. We end up not living to our full capabilities, and the potential and the gifts we have remain buried inside us. This is the danger of trying to follow someone else and wanting to be like them. We each have our own talents and areas we are good at. This means that we should not compare ourselves with another human being because we do not have any reason to do this. Each one of us is unique and irreplaceable. Society tells us some people have it all figured out and so we must be like them, and we must follow those who are successful and appear well-off in this life. But those people are not you! You are different. I love the fact that there is no one like me in this world! No one has the same exact fingerprint as I do. No one in the world is exactly like you! This is authenticity. This is the most precious thing you hold about who you are.

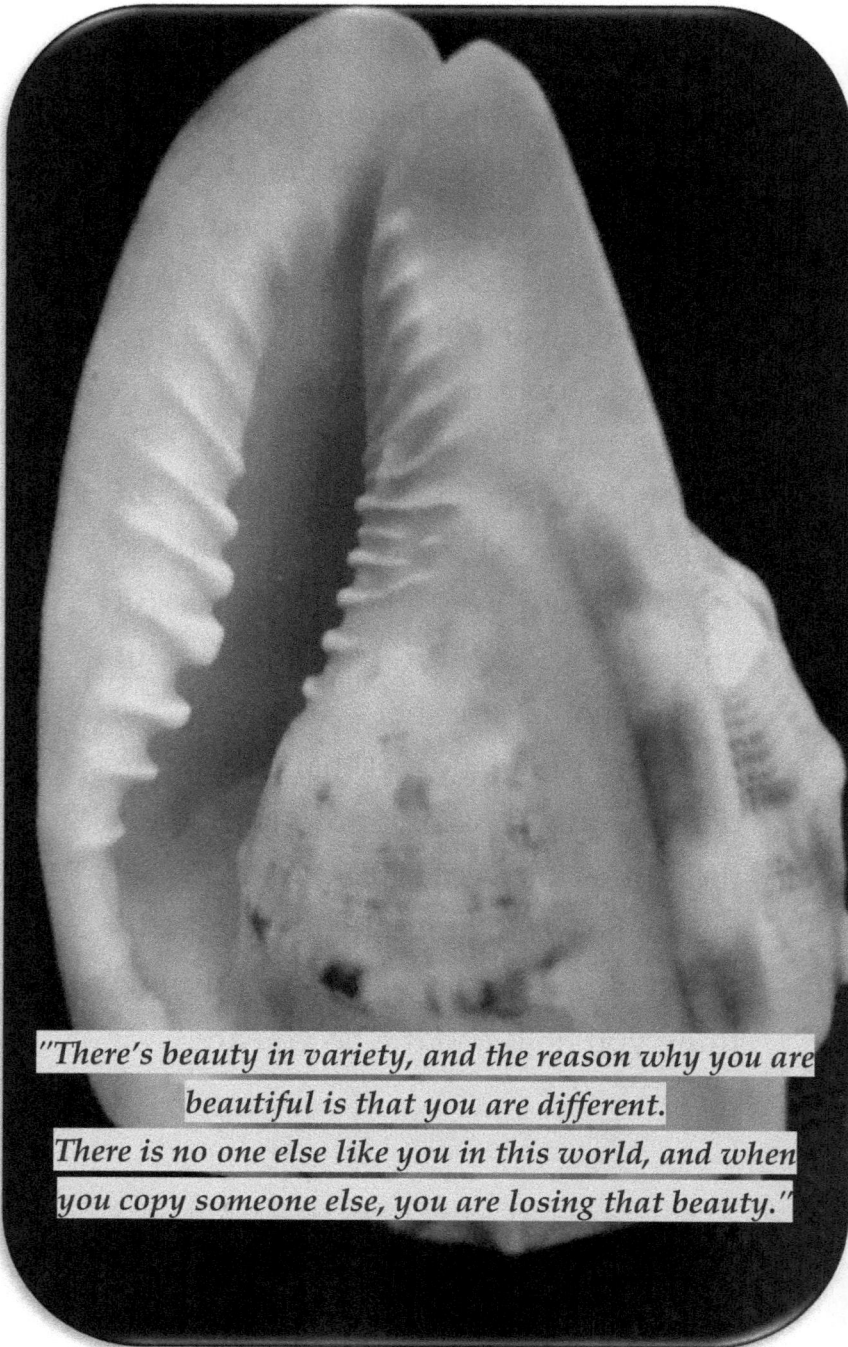

"There's beauty in variety, and the reason why you are beautiful is that you are different.
There is no one else like you in this world, and when you copy someone else, you are losing that beauty."

12.

It all boils down to one thing

Few things in life are worth dying for. If we try to peel off the layers of what is important to us, there will not be much left. All the superficial things will go. The material things and stuff we surround ourselves with for our comfort and convenience will peel away. Prestige and honor will be traded for the ones we love. Luxury and affluence in life and even power over other people will not matter. What's left will be our relationships. It all boils down to this one thing.

If you ask yourself what is the one thing you will save when there is a fire in your home, what will it be? Don't we immediately think of our loved ones only? We never think of our possessions when the situation is life and death. We only cling to life. We hold on to our life and the lives of those we love.

It all boils down to this one thing, our relationships. When everything is said and done, we realize that only one thing is of value and that is life itself. Life without all the beautiful things we thought life needed and so we spent our lifetime to possess. Life consists of you being alive and your loved ones. Their lives matter. It all boils down to this. The relationship we keep with those who give our life meaning and purpose.

First is your relationship with your Creator to whom we owe everything including life itself. God is important and so we must guard our relationship with Him. Our relationship with God is what gives meaning to our existence. If this is missing in your life, you will be continuously searching for "something" to fill in that empty 'void" inside your heart. But this is a God-shaped vacuum, this emptiness you sometimes feel inside your soul can only be filled with God. He planted eternity in the human heart and the problem is that we search for Him in all the wrong places. Many people try to fill in this void with what this world is offering, such as wealth, relationships, prestige, religions, drugs, or sex. But nothing can ever satisfy this longing inside our hearts. Only Jesus Christ can satisfy your soul.

Second is our relationship with the important people in our lives. Your spouse, children, parents, brothers, and sisters. Then you have your friends and family relatives. People are more important than all the material possessions we have. These things make us happy for a time but they never last. They never really fulfill us. Even a successful career never makes us fully satisfied. There remains a longing inside of us even if we reach the pinnacle of success. What is this longing? Our longings to make a difference are innate in all of us. There is something inside us that wants to matter. To serve a purpose bigger than life. We long for our life to count. With this, we know we are not here to merely exist. We have a higher purpose than just to live to eat and drink. There is more to life than all these.

What gives life meaning? When we are serving our purpose life becomes meaningful. We have a reason to live. It gives our life meaning. Our life's purpose has seasons. When starting a family, young parents' purpose in life can be to raise good children. Alongside this, we build relationships with our friends and the community around us. As a young person, one needs to learn and develop life skills to prepare them for the future. This is the reason why we go to school and training centers so we can be productive members of the society we live in. Those who are just starting out their careers are at the prime season of life. This is the season when one is passionate and driven. This is the time to build dreams and achieve them. This is also the time most people search for life's meaning and purpose. A season of trial and error until one finds their place in the universe. It is a season of excitement and lots of defeats and failures mixed with some success. Then the closing season, which is like the autumn time when most people in their late fifties prepare for retirement. Most years have gone by and like the falling autumn leaves, only a few are left as the beautiful color of this change of season is displayed in each leaf's color. Similarly, each of the stories of our lives in this season of life will emerge beautifully as we look back to what we have done in life. Then when retirement comes, like the winter season, we are hopefully prepared from our years of preparation. The autumn season is a preparation for the arrival of winter. Most of the root vegetables are being harvested around this time in readiness to give warmth during the cold and dark winter months. The winters of life can also be one of the joys of living. I love winter because of the snow. Though I don't really like the cold very much, I love watching the crisp, icy mornings of winter. Old age is one of the most interesting seasons of our lives. This is the time when we resign ourselves to all the pressures and demands of life. Most of those in this season couldn't care less whether they wear the right color of socks or whether their necktie is the appropriate design to match their shirt! I love listening to the stories of my patients when they tell me about their youth and what they have done in life. There are many amazing feats and adventures written all over their faces. I can see the delight in their eyes whenever they tell me their most unforgettable moments. A lot of times, these were the moments they spent with their kids or their grandkids when they took them out to the zoo or when they went skiing with them in the Alps. I can't remember any of them ever mentioning about becoming the CEO of their company or the time when they have been awarded an honor, though some of them were really decorated people full of great achievements in life! The moments they can't forget were those times they spent helping others, or being with the people they love the most.

People important to us matter more than our drive for success and accumulation of wealth. We have to remember this as we live our lives. It is very easy to be caught up with the hustle and bustle of life. When we are very busy and living life in the fast lane, it is easy to forget what is truly important. You can get swept away by it. In the end, you can lose sight of what matters in your life. Don't let this happen to you. Stop and evaluate your life. Try to peel off the layers before they overwhelm you. Slow down and take time to observe and analyze where your life is heading. Is this where you want to be in ten or twenty years? When you look back, would you be happy with what you will see?

"It all boils down to this one thing, our relationships.
When everything is said and done, we realize that only one thing is of value and that is life itself."

13.

Finding meaning in the midst of the mundane

How do you make your everyday existence count for something greater than your life? How do you live with a purpose in the routines of life? Finding meaning in what you do at work, school, or at home is something we all need to learn. I personally want to do something special each day, something out of the ordinary and beyond the routines of my daily life. To live with a purpose each day, you need to make a conscious effort to live for something even while you are doing the daily tasks. I tend to consciously stop if needed for someone who needs help. I try to take my time to notice someone who might need a helping hand on the way to work, for example. Maybe a neighbor needs someone to listen to after a hard day at work? What about during office time when a colleague is struggling or is in need of someone who can listen to their story? It's not easy but it can be done. I remember sleeping much better and having a smile on my face every time my day ended with a good deed or a good talk with someone who needed it most.

To find meaning in the midst of the mundane, you have to try to be conscious of wanting to make your day mean something. It is a choice we must make each day. This will help prepare you for a day that will be different from the ordinary days you have.

Here are three steps to take to make your seemingly ordinary routine become meaningful:

Stop for someone, be it an old lady who needs assistance with her shopping or crossing the road, or a friend who desperately needs someone to talk to. Be there and be in the moment with someone. Do not be afraid to get your routine interrupted. Stop for people in need. You will sleep better, and you will end the day with a smile on your face.

Take time to notice beauty, wherever it is, appreciate beauty. It might be in the face of your daughter or the gentle, thoughtful gesture of your spouse. Learn to appreciate it. Beauty is all around us. The flowers you see and the colors of trees when they change in autumn can bring joy to our hearts. Take time to smell the flowers or listen to the waves of the ocean. Notice beauty all around you. There is so much beauty in nature and in people. We must train our eyes to look for beauty. Fill your day with things you can appreciate rather than criticize. It's all in your eyes and what you choose to pay attention to. Make each day count by appreciating all the beauty it has to offer.

Be open to change. Change is good. Even in our routines, we must welcome any change or interruptions because it might open new doors or opportunities.

Instead of being upset when change comes to your daily schedule, be excited about it and see what new things can come out of it. Look at every change as an opportunity. Learn to be thankful even if things are not going your way. Life is an adventure and the only way you can be excited about life is when new things are happening around you. Learn to embrace change and setbacks. They can turn into something you have been looking for. Who knows?

Try to be happy every day. Enjoy each moment. No matter how routine your life can be, there is always something to be happy about in your daily life. Appreciate the smell of your morning coffee. Smile at the sunrise or even the rain! You won't appreciate the sun without the rain! Always smile at people. You never know who is going through hard times. Your smile can help lighten their load. Be gentle to others. **Speak slowly and listen carefully and patiently**. People appreciate a great listener. End your day with joy. Make it count by always being there for someone who needs you. Doing these will help you find meaning even in the midst of the mundane. It is not hard to attempt to brighten up someone's day by smiling or offering a helping hand. Sometimes a kind word or a cheerful encouragement can do wonders for a struggling colleague. Make your everyday an extraordinary day!

"Do not be afraid to have your routines interrupted. Stop for people in need. You will sleep better and end the day with a smile on your face."

14.

Beauty out of the ashes

Nature shows us time and time again how beauty can emerge out of complete ruins. We see this in the aftermath of super typhoons. The air feels cleaner, and peace comes after the devastation it brought. Life is not immune to setbacks and suffering. Everyone could go through some kind of trouble or trials, but the main thing is what these untoward events can teach us. Going through hardships can train us to be patient and more tolerant. It can also help us develop our character. It is like refining gold or silver. These precious metals go through fire to purify them and get them to shine and sparkle. We also emerge as stronger people after life's trials and hardships. We won't be able to develop a beautiful character and disposition unless we go through these difficulties in life. Let us be thankful for even the most untoward situations in our lives. We will never know the beauty that can come out of the ashes of tragedy and pain. A Holocaust survivor named Corrie Ten Boom was a Dutch lady who helped hide several Jews in Amsterdam during the time of the Nazis. She eventually was imprisoned for this and was sent to a concentration camp along with her sister. They lost their parents too. Her sister died shortly after. She found herself having to struggle alone for survival. She saw unimaginable brutality. Yet in the face of great evil, she chose to love even the perpetrators of evil in front of her. She refused to be changed by the darkness around her. She chose to stay in the light. She did not let her circumstances turn her into an evil person. She chose to forgive her enemies. She chose to love them instead. After the Holocaust, she found herself among those who survived. She emerged victorious and beautiful in character and as a person. She traveled around the world speaking about the power of love in the face of great evil. She saw beauty out of the ashes.

When confronted with difficulties and trials, we oftentimes try to shrink away from the pain and hurt they will leave in our hearts. But these same blows are what make our lives perfect. I love the quote about The Chisel, which C. S. Lewis, a Christian writer, once said: "You see, we are like blocks of stone out of which the Sculptor carves the forms of men. The blows of his chisel, which hurt us so much, are what make us perfect." No matter how painful the blows of these traumas are, if we allow the sculptor to work his way in us, we will be a work of art after these. These are what will help shape our character, strengthen our faith, and deepen our love for God. It is through these experiences that we get to know God more and understand His mysterious ways. When we look back at all these trials, we will be thankful not just for the lessons learned but for what it has left within our soul. Trust the hand of God, though sometimes difficult. There will always be something beautiful that will come out of this pain. We cannot always see what God can see as we go through trials in life. It is easier to choose to look at the negative side of what we are experiencing; the pain and the sorrows of life can be amplified a thousand times when we keep on repeating the thoughts and memories of these events in our minds. But if we try to look at what God can see, we can find the courage to hang on. In her poem, Corrie Ten Boom mentioned that life in God's hands is like a tapestry. Oftentimes we only see the beautiful picture, but God sees the underside of the picture; though the weavings are everywhere and messy, those are what made the picture beautiful. God, in His sovereign will, can permit untoward events in our lives to make through them a beautiful picture of our lives. He even promises to work all things out for our good in the end, though sometimes we make bad choices in life. He is a good and loving God who keeps watch over the issues of your life. Don't ever think for a second that He doesn't know what you are going through. Sometimes, in the midst of despair, we only need to trust the loving hand of our God. He will see you through it all. After the storm has passed, you will emerge stronger than before. Your life will show forth the beauty that comes out of the ashes!

Life is but a weaving

My life is but a weaving
Between my God and me.
I cannot choose the colors
He weaveth steadily.

Oft times He weaveth sorrow;
And I in foolish pride
Forget He sees the upper
And I the underside.

Not til the loom is silent
And the shuttles cease to fly
Will God unroll the canvas
And reveal the reason why.

The dark threads are as needful
In the weaver s skillful hand
As the threads of gold and silver
In the pattern He has planned

He knows, He loves, He cares;
Nothing this truth can dim.
He gives the very best to those
Who leave the choice to Him.

-Corrie ten Boom

"Life is not immune to setbacks and suffering. Everyone could go through some kind of trouble or trials, but the main thing is what these untoward events can teach us."

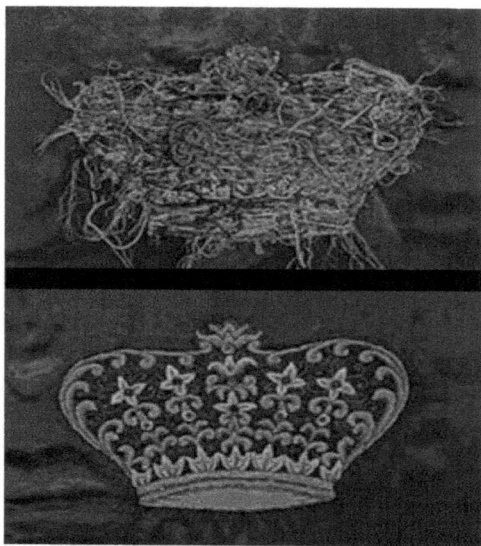

15.

Living life to the fullest

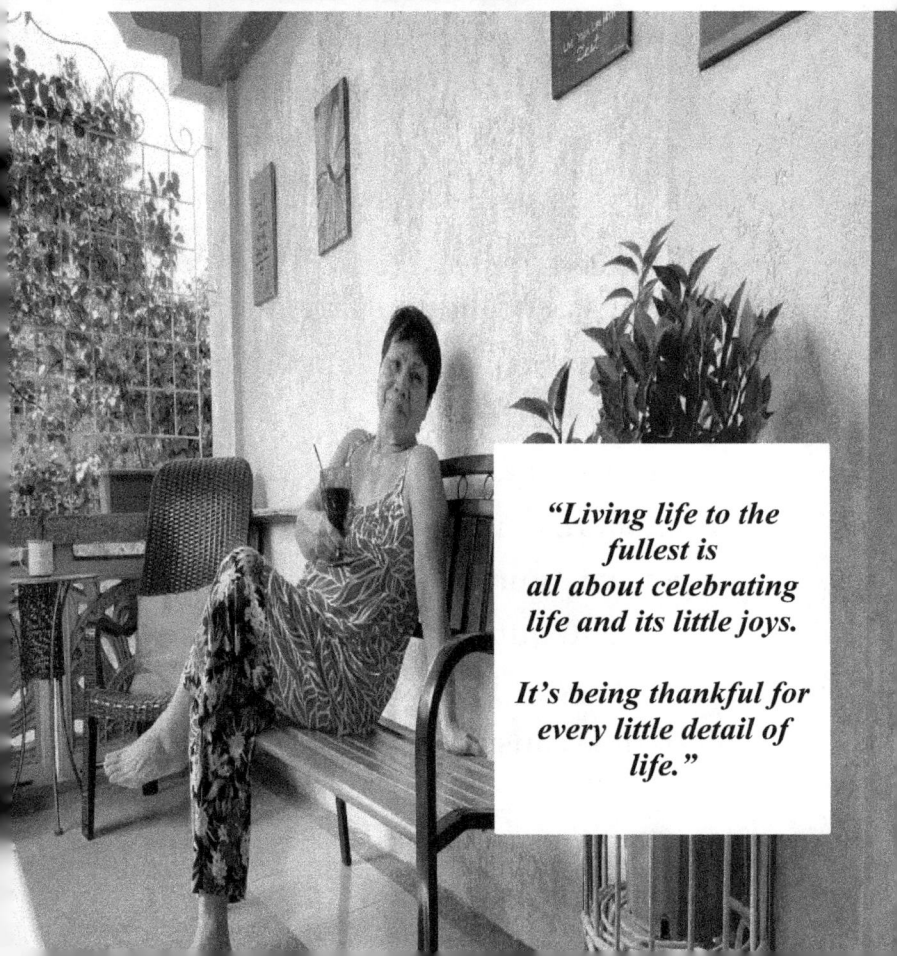

"Living life to the fullest is all about celebrating life and its little joys.

It's being thankful for every little detail of life."

How do you make your life meaningful? How do you live a full life in everyday routines that seem too mundane, too ordinary? I see life as a new beginning every day, a new opportunity, a fresh start to do something worthwhile. I strive each day to make a difference in the lives of others around me, no matter how small. It can be just a smile to a lonely stranger, or offering unexpected help to someone who does not expect anything. A listening ear offered to a friend in need, and a tap on the shoulder of a struggling father, can go a long way. We can never know the impact our lives are making on others. But the most important thing is not to know or measure it, but to deliberately make an effort to do it. Life is meaningless without causing change for the betterment of society. Life means something only when you are making a difference in the life of a child, a mother, a father, or even a complete stranger.

Living life to the fullest is all about celebrating life and its little joys. It's being thankful for every detail of life: the air in our lungs, and the light in our eyes that enable us to see beauty are things we can always be grateful for. If we wake up with an attitude of thankfulness and appreciation each day, we will start it with joy and positive energy. That can make an impact on the people around us. Smile and appreciate what you see in the mirror. Keep a journal of positive thoughts and reflections. Be the first to greet a stranger. Be the one who offers a helping hand to a colleague at work.

Savor life and experience it with gratitude and passion. Don't let it just pass you by. Taste it and enjoy each moment of the 24 hours allotted to you each day. Life is too short to waste it on negative thoughts and worrying about something you do not know will even come in your tomorrow. Live and enjoy the moment. Be present in every conversation with a friend or a loved one. Turn your mobile phone off and do not let it interfere with your time with the most important people in your life. It is never life and death not to answer the phone or reply to a message. Give yourself a break from technology. Life is not all about what social media tells you it is. Go outside and experience the beauty of nature around you. Listen to the sound of the waves, walk barefoot on the sand, and allow yourself to meditate on the goodness of God in your life. There is always something to be thankful for, and that is what you must look for at the start and end of each day. I love the analogy of a Brazilian poet named Mario de Andrade in his poem entitled "My Soul is in a Hurry." He uses the analogy of the years of his life to that of a bowl of cherries. At first, the child gulped and ate the cherries without thought, thinking there were loads of cherries in his bowl. But then slowly there were only a few cherries left in the bowl. The little boy then started to slowly eat and taste each cherry one at a time, savoring it because there were not many left. Life is sometimes like this. When life has been spent and youth is gone, then we start to realize we have fewer and fewer years to spend in life. There were more years spent already as we look back and very few left when we look forward to our future years. Life is indeed so short. How we live today matters tomorrow. His poem is to the point and touches on the everyday scenario of life. Most importantly, he helps us to see life as a one-time opportunity, here today, and gone tomorrow.

No matter how one thinks life is so mundane, there is always an opportunity each day to make life meaningful. To enjoy life and appreciate all it offers is a good start. Then, go out of your way and look for something outside of yourself as the next step. Notice other people. Be sensitive to their needs. See how you can make a difference and do it gladly.

Make your life meaningful by being present in each moment of your life.

Celebrating life includes the little moments when you allow yourself to experience the joy of helping others. Life is short and there is only one life for each of us to live. If we live in the moment, we can learn to appreciate every little thing in this life. We can appreciate the beauty of each day with what nature is showing us, we can hear and cherish the sound of our children's voices and the soft whisper of those whose hearts have loved us. Take time to notice life's little joys. If you do, you will discover that there are plenty of these around. Life indeed can be celebrated every day! And most of these are free and no amount of money can ever buy them!

16.

The curse of materialism

Materialism is like a cancer in our society. It creeps into our lives from a young age. Remember the countless toys we used to have fun with? Those Barbie doll collections and the Lego toys from Toys R Us? Every Christmas, our mom and dad would surround us with the latest gadgets and stuff we would use for a few weeks before they found their way into the attic. Then, as we started going out with our friends, we learned to compare cool stuff, like the latest iPhone or drone, game console, or the coolest outfit on the high street. We did this like clockwork every season. Then we started to have our own money. We began to work and have our own buying power. In came the relentless need to accumulate and buy things we didn't really need. We collected things we only used once or twice. We tried to have stuff we saw on Facebook because our neighbors or friends had them. We filled our houses with so many things that we ran out of space to put them. Shopping became an addiction. Getting upgrades became a necessity. Ours is a society of throwing away and replacing. We lost the ability to repair and reuse things. We wanted new things even if we didn't really need them. Materialism can be overwhelming. It silently robs us of what is truly precious to us. What is more important? Things or health? People or phones? When we feel pressured to have the same upgrades as the rest of our friends, we become the subject of what they call "the curse" of materialism. You go about your life oblivious to the fact that you accumulate material things not because you need them, but because you unconsciously just want to fit in. To fit in the society you are in, you have to be like the rest of them. This is the curse of materialism, and it will consume your life until you die if you do not stop and break free from its hold.

Materialism has silently crept into every generation in many Western societies. The more advanced life has become, the more bitter the curse that comes with it. The appeal of materialism can be very subtle. It flashes on your phone's screen like innocent entertainment. It conditions your mind to want something or feel the need to acquire something you don't really need. It comes to you, attempting to tempt you to possess them and to be "in" and to belong among the "more acceptable" crowds in your community. Peer pressure is very high among young people because this is what most advertising companies use to lure them to buy their products. The trend can be upgraded every season, and this becomes a constant wave of business streams promising unlimited profit for the corporate giants. On and on this cycle comes to us, tagging us along in this endless pursuit for things we don't really need. We end up working hard each day just to "afford" these suggested lifestyles and possessions. Before we know it, we have consumed our earnings buying things we normally throw away after mostly a year. But the hardest truth to swallow in this is that before we know it, our years are being consumed with this endless demand for material gain, leaving us broke and empty in the end.

How do you break free from materialism? To do this, you must be determined to let go of some of your accumulated stuff. The Japanese principle of a "minimalist lifestyle" will have to be your new resolution. Once a year, go over your material stuff and try to give away those you have already forgotten about, but are still occupying space in your house. You can make someone else happy by giving those forgotten stuff away instead. Check on your clothes, shoes, bags, toys, gadgets, books, etc. The aim is to try to only surround yourself with the things you love the most. The goal is to live with the minimal amount of stuff around you. Doing this will create more space in your house and will unconsciously give you a sense of freedom. You will feel that you can breathe again. Doing this every year will change your life.

Another step to take is to ask yourself, "Do I really need this?" before buying anything. Most of the time, we just become victims of false advertisements. It conditions our minds and convinces us we need something even though we don't. So, next time you find yourself in a shopping spree, stop and ask the question: "Do I really need this?"

Think about whether the stuff you are accumulating will have a lasting impact on your life. Most of these are temporary and won't last. Alexander the Great had these wishes upon his death. He asked that his coffin be carried only by the top physicians of his time to show the world that at the time of death, even the best physicians were helpless. He also asked that the road towards the cemetery be covered with his wealth and possessions to show the world that anything acquired on earth stays on earth. No one takes anything with them in death.

Surround yourself only with the things you love. Those which give you peace and remind you of your happy moments. Discard and give away the rest. This practice will lighten your load in life. You will feel so free and light after doing this. I promise you won't regret trying to do this radical but important step to break free from the hold of materialism in your life. I challenge you to be free now and enjoy more of your remaining years!

"Once a year, go over your material stuff and try to give away those you have already forgotten but are still occupying space in your house.
You can make someone else happy by giving those forgotten stuff away instead."

17.

The pull of the "visible"

How does our attention to the temporary and the visible rob us of more permanent things in this life? The tyranny of the "urgent" demands our constant obedience every day. Our "to do" list is a testament to how we are inclined to succumb to its bidding rather than take our time to pause and consider what is more important. The call of the daily necessities is louder. The bills we have to pay and the pressure of society to follow the "almost laid out" paths for us to take are stronger. But what is truly important in life is set aside, and the temporary, "visible," and "urgent" things take centre stage. Before we know it, our years are gone, and when we look back, we cannot remember the time when we stopped and did what we really wanted to do in this life.

Regret is the most painful word. It spells those days that turned into years when we chose to postpone what is more important in order to attend to "urgent" matters. After all, the laundry has been waiting for a week or the emails are piling up and need to be answered! Every day, these seemingly "urgent" tasks call our attention and demand that we do them! We must learn to say no to these and evaluate what needs to be done according to their importance. You may not see the impact of the seemingly wasted time you spent with your kids, parents, or your friends, but those are the ones that will last. The warmth of friendship never goes away. This invisible difference your life is making to the lives of your children and those around you may not be "visible" to you, but these are more permanent. Yet, we tend to trade them for the temporary. We get busy with the everyday routines, pursue our careers to get ahead in this life, and to provide all the material stuff for our loved ones. But in the process, we lose them. We can exchange the much-needed time with them for the high-pressure jobs we thought we needed to buy them the stuff we thought makes them happy. What lasts are not the material things we give them but the quality time we spend with those we love the most in this life.

What will be your regrets in life? Think about the end, when you are already at your deathbed. What would be the things you would have wished you would have done? Start doing those "regrets" now while you still have the chance. While your parents are still alive, do everything for them that you would have wished you had done for them. Say what you would have wished you said, do it now. Because tomorrow may not come for you.

Each day, when you look at your "to do" list, think about which one of those is going to leave a lasting impact in your life. What are the urgent ones but not important? What are the ones you tend to take for granted because you can't see its   effect   immediately?

Don't let the tyranny of the urgent enslave you. You are the one in charge of your life. You can make choices that will impact your destiny and make a difference in the lives of the people important to you. Don't let the visible things rob you of them. Start creating memories with them. Live your life and treat it as a journey to be enjoyed with those you love. Appreciate everything around you. Do not be in a hurry all the time. Learn the art of slowing down and and, if necessary, have the courage to stop and begin again.

*"Regret is the most painful word.
It spells those days that turned into
years when we chose to postpone what
is more important in order to attend to
'urgent' matters."*

18.

Living in the moment

The power of being present lies in the fact that we value every single moment in this life knowing that we could not have the same moments twice. When we realize this, we will start to cherish each of our moments and learn to be present. To be present is to be "in the moment". Have you ever noticed how, because of our obsession with social media, we are "losing" these precious moments? How many times have you observed a couple or a family inside a restaurant, attempting to bond and build a special time together, yet they were all staring at their phone screens and not really talking to each other? Moments when they could have been creating memories and enjoying each other can be turned into a meaningless get together because we lost our ability to be "present" in the moment. Sometimes, we just "scroll" through our moments and not really take our time to "savor" them and enjoy its beauty. Every day, we quickly "scroll" through each moment without thinking and we "lose" its significance in the process.

Understanding why God has asked us to rest and take His yoke because it is light and easy is key to knowing how to be present. Jesus said to come to Him when we are weary and tired and to take His yoke because His yoke is easy, and His burden is light. What does he mean by this? He meant that learning to enter his rest will teach us to be more aware, to learn of Him, the power of living each day, not worrying about tomorrow. Learning to be present. Learning to be "in the moment".

Learning to Behold

Sometimes, all God asked from us is to learn to behold. Behold each moment He is giving us. Behold each experience, behold each beauty, each blessing, each joy. We must not rush on to the next day. This moment right now is all we have. When we lose this

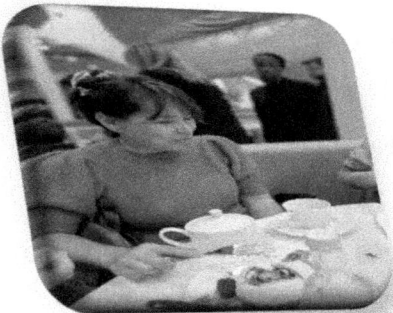

ability to just cherish each moment, we rush and run in life. We miss the many things we should behold at each stop. Learning to behold is like what faith is. Faith is a "gaze" of our soul to the "One" who has saved us from ourselves, from our sin, our sinful nature. Jesus Christ is the focus, the center of this gaze. In one of my blogs, I wrote about learning to live in the moment. My friend from Canada sent me a note to say how she remembered a time when she was being given a beautiful moment to see a blue jay bird and to her excitement went out to get her camera so she can show the picture to her kids. But when she returned, the bird had gone! It was the first time ever she has seen one and it was beautiful! She felt the Lord said: "That was just for you, behold these moments." I thought it was so beautiful. To behold our moments. Sometimes God just wants us to behold. When John the Baptist saw Jesus coming towards him, he said to the people following him; "Behold the Lamb of God". To behold means to see or to not miss something. Here is something we must not miss. When we look at something we could be looking at it but miss it. It means to not really see what we are looking at! We are missing what our eyes are beholding at a given moment. Faith is a gaze of our soul to the one true God. At this instance, we learn to see God, see His beauty and splendor. We have believed. When Moses raised the pole with the bronze snake on it, the people who had been bitten by a snake and looked at the bronze snake lifted by Moses on the pole were all healed and saved from the snake bite. What does this teach us? All of us who looked on Jesus, who behold His face, know the faith that He authored in our hearts the moment we believed and looked upon Him. To behold His face is all He asked. Sometimes we get so preoccupied with many things in this life. Remember the story of Martha and Mary? When Jesus visited their house, he came to Martha's house to visit her. But Martha's younger sister was there, and she did a remarkable thing. One that was recorded in the Bible. What she did was singled out by Jesus. Martha was preoccupied about the housework and preparations. But Mary sat at Jesus feet and listened to His words. Martha was not happy because her sister was not helping her with the housework. Jesus told her: "Martha, you are so worried about so many things but only one thing is needful, and Mary has chosen this, and it will not be taken away from her".

Sometimes all that's needed is to behold. Life can be busy, and you ended up doing a lot of things when all God wants you to do is to behold... behold the beauty of each moment He is giving you, behold His words to you, His goodness, His mercy. Sometimes, when life is busy, we just "scroll" through our moments and we miss their meaning. Learn to behold. When you are worried and tired, God calls you to rest, He don't demand anything from you. Sometimes all that's needed is to behold His face.

19.

The Balancing Act of Stone Stacking

The art of stone stacking is very intriguing. My brother Arman is an avid mountain climber, and he said this is something most climbers do on every climb. He also created a beautiful lineup of stone stacking displays along a path by our house, and I was very impressed with it. My father, curious about how the stones were sticking together, moved one of the stackings and it fell apart just as fast as he touched them! To his amazement, my brother, with his expert hands, managed to put them back together so quickly in perfect balance! My father was amazed at how the stones looked like they had been glued together when the only thing holding them together is their balancing act! Have you ever noticed the same thing with your life? How life feels more peaceful and relaxed when you have a balanced schedule? What I mean by this is that if you don't overwhelm your schedule each day, it feels like you have it all together, isn't it?

Balance is an elusive concept. Many of us try to have balance in our life only to fall short of arriving at such a perfect state of rest and peace. Balance in life is all around us if we learn to observe nature. Nature is the perfect display of what balance looks like. Watch the trees as they silently find their way in the forest, balancing each other in the process called symbiosis. The ocean balances the weather every day. The low tide and high tide influence the balance of rain and wind, providing the perfect and harmonious habitat for all the fish and sea creatures thriving inside this world. We see balance in the life of each flower as they bloom and how they work together among the bees and garden insects to create just the right balance for each of their species to live. Balance is key to peaceful existence. Life can be very exhausting if we don't know that balance comes naturally if only, we let nature take its course. How do we learn balance from nature? Watching a spider knit its web, which will be its home for the night, can be very exhilarating. This tiny creature will intricately build its home without caring about the next day when it will be completely squashed by passersby, blown by the wind, or trampled by another bigger insect. Spiders are ready to rebuild their home again and again. Such tenacity! But such a balanced act of learning to accept the way they are made! They learn to work with whatever lot they were given. If we will learn balance in life, this is the first thing we need to learn. To accept where we landed in life. To embrace our present moment and learn to thrive in it with joy. To learn to dance to the tune of life. To learn to flow and move according to the wind's direction. This, we can learn from the way bamboos joyfully sway along with the wind no matter how strong the winds are. They learn to sway, dance, and move according to the blow of the wind and therefore, even if it's a strong typhoon and the battering is too much, you'll see bamboos emerge undefeated after the storm! Why? They know the secret of balance and that is to flow with the wind. They dance and follow in its direction. They don't resist the wind. They bow if needed or dance with it if needed. Learn balance from nature around you. Take time to notice its beauty and watch its balancing act. Then bring that balance into your own life.

If you notice how seasons change, you'll know that it is nature's way of balancing our atmosphere. Summer brings heat and dryness and the sun in its fullness, and we see all the trees and the plants blooming and thriving at their best. But then comes the fall when all the leaves will die and slowly fall off, preparing them for winter. We see the beauty of this change by the arrays of beautiful yellow and orange hues on display. This change is giving balance to the life of each tree and plant, allowing them to recuperate. Then we see the winter when the whole of nature seems to hide from us. Snow comes and gives us a sense of joy in the middle of dark days. But spring comes and the refreshing smell of blossoms and the colourful tulips start to smile at us telling us, the balancing act of nature has all been completed and so new life starts to begin again. Life is like seasons. It knows how to balance itself. We should not resist any change, but we should learn to understand what it teaches us at each season. The Bible teaches that in everything there is a season, and a time for every matter under heaven.

Every season of life is meant to add beauty and strength to our life. We must learn to read between the lines. Each season is important and necessary. The change it brings is good for us. The main thing is that nothing in life is permanent, like the seasons, it will change. If we learn to live in each season of life, appreciating the beauty it brings to us, then we have found balance, and this will help take us farther in our life's journey.

"Life is like seasons. It knows how to balance itself. We should not resist any change, but we should learn to understand what it teaches us at each season."

20.

Finding meaning at the end of it all

━━━━━━━━━━

I once gave a special person one of my favorite paintings that I painted on a stretched canvas using oil and acrylic colors. This was the first time I used these mixed media, and I was very thrilled that it worked! It was beautiful, and I loved it, but I had to give it away. While I was packing the picture, I thought of what to write on the back as a little note. This person was very successful in life. What can I say to someone who has achieved so much in life and maybe got everything they want? A simple wish was all I could think of, and I wrote: "May you find meaning at the end of it all."

At the end of our struggles, dreams, and success, what is left for us to wish for? What else is there for us to do? One of my privileges as a professional nurse is that I get to witness people in their last days of life. I had this rare opportunity to look through a dying patient's eyes and gaze into their soul. I remembered one of these occasions early on in my nursing career when I was holding a dying patient's hands. There, on his deathbed, uttering his last few words, I saw the most unforgettable look which will be forever etched in my heart. He said, "I don't want to die... I haven't done what I was supposed to do in my life..." There, I saw for the first time the painful look of regret in this man's eyes. It stayed with me for the rest of my life. I was twenty-eight years old. That was the day I decided to pack my bags and set out to do what I knew my life was supposed to do in this life. I told myself, I don't want to be on my deathbed and regret that I have not done what I was supposed to do in my life. I left my job and went to a missionary training center the following month. I knew what my life was supposed to do. I would spend my years serving others and making a difference even in the lives of nameless, insignificant children roaming the dark streets of Asia. I survived the horrors of what I saw by cherishing each life. Though sometimes it is hard to continue because I always wonder whether I am making any difference at all to the situation of millions of these children, I always tell myself it made a difference to the life of each child saved. It made a difference to that one life. Because of this, it is all worth it. I once read about the Starfish story which helped me see what I was doing in a different perspective. It was a story of a child walking along the beach after a terrible storm which washed up thousands of starfish. The child is throwing starfish back into the water, when someone admonishes the child that they cannot save them all, cannot really make a difference. The child picks up another and replies, "I made a difference to that one." Each time one life is saved from the hands of the traffickers, I would take one starfish and return it to the ocean!

In many of the Holocaust museums and

memorials which I visited in Europe and the United States, I remember one particular phrase from the Talmud which has left a lasting impression on me. It simply said: "He who saves a life, saves the world entire." Perhaps your life is only making an impact on one or two or perhaps a few more or many other lives. Remember, each one life is equivalent to the whole world. Did not Jesus say, "What shall it profit a man if he shall gain the whole world but loses his own soul? Or what shall a man give in exchange for his soul?

How do we find meaning in the life we have lived? What is the meaning of our brief existence? I believe that in order to find the answer to this probing question, we have to look deeper into our hearts and try to find our whys doing what we did or are still doing in this life.

Without the answer to the "whys," there is no meaning in what we do. It is in finding the whys that we get the meaning of our endeavors. Once we know this, we will begin to truly live. Living a life on purpose is key to knowing how to live. This is also the meaning of our death. When our life cycle ends, we find its meaning in the whys of our lives. That's when you find meaning at the end of it all.

God knows what He's doing when He requires us of this seemingly impossible pursuit of dying to self. Human nature is and always will be selfish. It is in dying to self, where one truly finds meaning at the end of it all. It is the only way to truly understand the meaning of life and your place in the universe and to truly live.

Jesus explicitly said He who loses his life will find it and he who saves his life will lose it. It is the meaning of life found in recklessly and completely abandoning your own life for the sake of giving it off for others to live.

Jesus said to all those who are weary and are heavy laden in this life to come to Him. He specifically said that His yoke is easy, and His burden is light. If we look at His life and examine how He lived it, it was because He gave off Himself for others that His life's meaning was found. It was by losing His life that He was able to impart life to us for our salvation. His mission in life was to die for our sins so that we could live. He said that greater love has no man than this; that a man lay down his life for his friend. He did the greatest act of love by dying for us, His enemies! Our sins have separated us from God. We have chosen our own way and rebelled against His will, choosing rather to be a friend of this world obeying its biddings. The Bible says friendship with the world is enmity with God and whosoever therefore will be a friend of the world is the enemy of God (James 4:4).

This principle should be championed in today's society where the pursuit of "self" has already become an obsession. It is in giving that we find joy and happiness that last. It is in what we give, not in what we keep, that our life's value is weighed.

This is really the Bible in a nutshell. Everything Christ said and did was selfless. Dying to self and losing life, all to find life itself.

This earthly life will never have a hold on anyone who finds this secret to living life. It makes one immune to the comings and goings of life. It teaches you to hold on to what truly matters in this life. You learn to be oblivious to what society dictates. You will learn to value things that last.

On Frustrations and Shattered Dreams

Most of us will need redemption even for the ideals we set in life which never materialized. We need to be broken and acceptance is key. We must find consolation in areas of our frustrations. When we are nearing the finish line, you and I will have to look back. At the end of the day, it is not really your achievements or whether you reached your ideals that matter in this life. It is whether you can find meaning at the end of all your endeavors. It is whether your life made a difference wherever you find yourself. By just accepting this and finding peace where we landed in life and accepting it and not comparing it against the high ideals which we unrealistically set for ourselves, or perhaps which society is trying to demand from us without even knowing, we can find our life's meaning there. I believe we can find meaning at every station in life we are in. All of us have impacted someone's life in one way or another. We need to see the small but significant difference we have made on another but not against the ideals we have set for ourselves to achieve but did not.

Life should not revolve around our dreams alone; that's not how we find meaning in this life. Many of those who have been successful and have attained their dreams and goals end up being so lonely and empty. Where do we find meaning and purpose? It's in the giving up of our own interest for the sake of another. It's ultimately in dying to self that we find life. This is the meaning we all are looking for at the end of our journey. Did my life matter to someone? Will I be remembered by others who have been on the same road as me in this life? Have I touched someone's life? Did my life resonate with another in their struggles and find hope and inspiration, knowing that they, too, can make it to the finish line because of my life's example?

The Pale Blue Dot

Nothing in all of creation has the power to ground anyone as the immense reality of the earth's insignificant size in comparison to the whole of the cosmos. The pale blue dot, famous as the space craft, Voyager's last photograph, taken as it left our own solar system, Voyager 1 was sent on a mission to take photographs of our solar system and the surrounding planets. Upon its return to Earth's orbit, the mission's manager asked the Voyager to take one last snapshot of the planet Earth as it left the solar system. This resulted in the now famous Pale Blue Dot, taken from around 3.7 billion miles away on February 14, 1990. The photo depicts Earth as a mote of dust suspended in a sunbeam. Carl Sagan, the American astronomer who popularized the famous photo of the pale blue dot, described the photograph this way: "The Earth looked like just a tiny mote of dust suspended in a sunbeam!"

How does this ground us? Looking at the size of the Earth from the viewpoint of the universe, we cannot even begin to grasp the enormous contrast of its size to the magnitude of the cosmos where it hangs. Knowing this puts our biggest worries into a comforting perspective; they are definitely insignificant compared to this scale. When one realizes this, maybe a shrinking feeling comes initially, but then, we also begin to appreciate how the Creator, in His amazing love for humanity, has placed so much value and importance on us. He has created us in His own image, and this is why we, humans, out of all creation, are the crown of His glory, the jewel of His majestic throne. Yet, in its profoundness, we come to understand that there is no reason on Earth to be proud, greedy, or to seek to conquer the whole of this tiny world. We know that this tiny planet hangs upon nothing in God's universe and is only the size of a tiny mote of dust, unseen in the darkness of the cosmos. How can one justify a thirst for power and a lifelong quest for riches and possessions, knowing that at any second, this tiny Earth can be hit by a wandering asteroid? It can lose its orbit at any time when the sun decides to change its course. Then, the Earth as we know it will be no more.

Every endeavour under the sun, if pursued with material profit or worldly success and pleasure in mind, is bound to leave one empty. We must realize the message of the pale blue dot so that we no longer have to join the rest in pursuing something that will eventually leave emptiness rather than enrich our soul.

It's amazing how, as you get closer to the realization of all your dreams, the less hold you have on them. It's surreal, but I guess you get to have a grasp of eternity this way, I mean of experiencing God and the possibilities of all impossibilities. When you see Him this way, it humbles you. One is left in awe of God.

To see life in this perspective is to discover its power to anchor our lives to the One who created all the wonders of the universe. One can only stand in awe of Him who created this immense universe and see in it the greatest manifestation of the glory of God. This is the power that can help ground a person to living a life with real meaning and purpose.

This should be everyone's ultimate journey! It's the only journey that leads to our understanding of our place in the universe—the answer to our existential question since the dawn of time—"Why are we here ?" Why do we exist, and why am I given the chance of life? The answer to this question lies in knowing where you came from and understanding why. It was said that there are two very important days in our life: the day we were born, and the day we found out why. What does this mean? When we were born, we were given one full chance of life. Finding out why we were born is the ultimate realization of life. The "why" behind what we are doing, the reason behind every endeavour is what gives meaning to our existence. It is why we wake up every morning, to fulfil our purpose, to do what we are born to do. With this, we will find meaning at the end of it all.

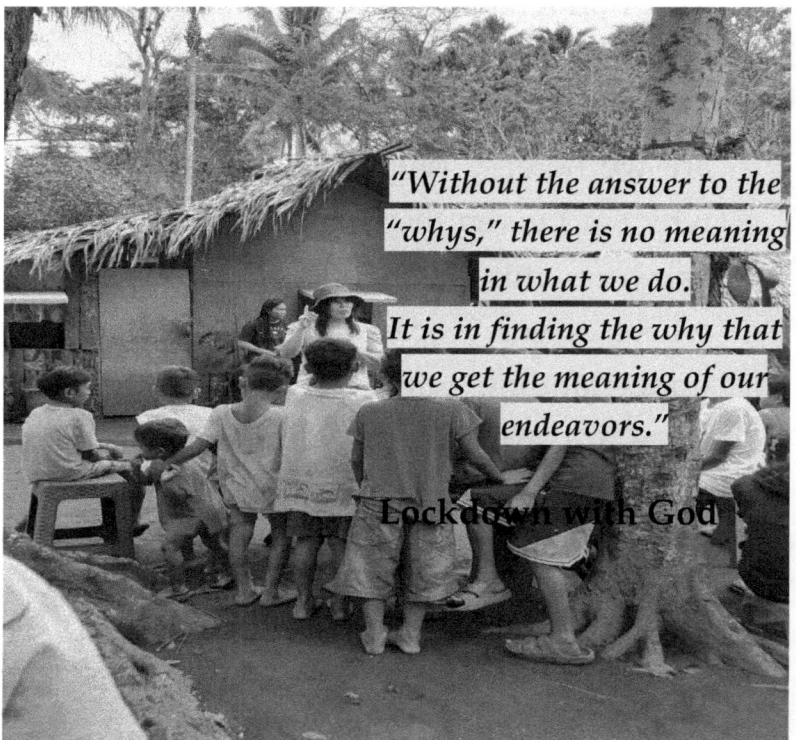

"Without the answer to the "whys," there is no meaning in what we do. It is in finding the why that we get the meaning of our endeavors."

Lockdown with God

ABOUT THE AUTHOR

Marivic is the founding missionary of North Korea & Beyond Missions International. She travels extensively as an itinerant Bible teacher and works with native pastors around the world to reach out to the most unreached people groups with the Gospel. She also speaks at churches and conferences worldwide. An anointed and gifted speaker, she brings the freshness of the Holy Spirit's presence whenever she preaches or teaches. She divides her time between overseas missions and working as a nurse in the United Kingdom. Additionally, she runs her own nursing agency business and enjoys painting and photography in her spare time. She loves taking long walks while listening to her favorite worship songs.

Notes

Reference for the UK 2021 Study on Loneliness, p. 34

Holt-Lunstad, J., Smith, T. B., Baker, M., Harris, T., & Stephenson, D. (2021). Loneliness and social isolation as risk factors for mortality: a meta-analytic review. Perspectives on Psychological Science, 10(2), 227-237.

Other Books by the Author

Lockdown with God
Finding your secret place

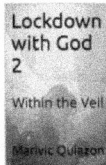

Lockdown with God 2
Within the veil

Lockdown with God 3
Devotional

Christian ?
Knowing who you are in Christ

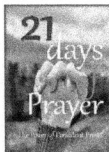

21 Days of Prayer
The power of persistent prayer

9 7 8 1 8 3 8 1 9 9 3 8 8